THE OAKWOOD PRESS

TAKEN BY TRAINS

The Life and Photographs of William Nash, 1909-1952

by
Kate Robinson & Robert Forsythe

© Oakwood Press & Kate Robinson 2004

British Library Cataloguing in Publication Data
A Record for this book is available from the British Library
ISBN 0 85361 619 1

Typeset by Oakwood Graphics.
Repro by Ford Graphics, Ringwood, Hants.
Printed by Cambrian Printers, Aberystwyth, Ceredigion.

Dedication

To father with thanks for leaving so many footsteps to follow – Kate

Front cover, foreground: William Nash's later camera, a Zeiss Ikon 6 x 9 cms format survives. It could be used with 120 roll film or glass plates. Nash favoured the former.

Rear cover: William Nash at 13, the year he started taking railway photographs.

Published by The Oakwood Press (Usk), P.O. Box 13, Usk, Mon., NP15 1YS.
E-mail: oakwood-press@dial.pipex.com
Website: www.oakwood-press.dial.pipex.com

Contents

Preface

It was a pleasant surprise to discover during the writing of my book *Harrow & Wealdstone, 50 years On: Clearing up the Aftermath* that the publisher, the Oakwood Press, also had in hand at the same time the production of a book of photographs, entitled *Cumbrian Railway Photographer, The William Nash Collection* taken by a victim of this horrific accident and were proposing to publish both books in the same month. This and subsequent discoveries were to confirm the adage 'The World gets smaller the older one becomes'.

I was to meet Kate Robinson later that year (2002), after my wife and I had viewed an exhibition in Penrith of her father's photographic work, whilst on our way north to stay with friends in the Borders. Then, not only did we discover that our two fathers had been born within not much more than a year of each other, but as teenage boys had attended Radley College, near Abingdon, at the same time, whilst prior to that William Nash had been to boarding school, in Guildford close to where I was brought up and in the area I have lived since. Being of an age and of similar upbringing it is not surprising that our fathers should both have done their bit to maintain normal life, as far as possible, during the General Strike in 1926 by volunteering to sign up, one as a temporary special constable to provide protection to the driver of a London bus, and the other to man a signal box. My father went on to become an architect, while Nash entered a professional career on the London, Midland & Scottish Railway Company (LMS) and subsequently the London Midland Region of British Railways.

It is with pleasure therefore that I commend to the reader the work of Kate Robinson and Robert Forsythe in their second joint venture in presenting to the public the photographs and story of Kate's father William Nash. As the sequel to *Cumbrian Railway Photographer*, this book, *Taken by Trains,* ventures more into the wider field of Britain's railways as a whole in the first half of the 20th century and covers all the main line companies, together with a number of narrow gauge lines. The accompanying text gives interesting insights into the life of a dedicated railwayman rising through middle management, who but for his tragic loss of life at Harrow, might have risen to greater things.

Peter Tatlow,
past Chairman of the LMS Society

Foreword

Albums of railway photographs are perhaps too common but in this publication by Kate Robinson and Robert Forsythe, based on the work of Kate's father, William Nash, we find something altogether different and refreshing. So often, photographs are produced which have no context or relevance off the page. But Kate Robinson has used her late father's collection to open a window into his life story. William Nash was interested in the railways and in photography. His interest in the former led to his finding a career on the railways and his interest in the latter found him taking time to record the railway scene. As his job moved him around the country or when he took a holiday away from home he would seek out the railway scene and, in particular, the local curiosities which were to be found within the between-the-wars railway network.

As a result this book offers an additional dimension to the reader. Nash's photographs are not simply a catalogue of trains observed. We follow a young man between the wars, initially as a schoolboy enthusiast, and then as his career commences and develops. It was a career that took him to new places, as it was for many on the railways. We can imagine him as a stranger in a new town, living in digs and passing time by exploring the local railway with his camera. Does a sense of the loneliness of the newly transferred officer come through in some of these photographs of the passing train in the countryside?

A young William Nash with his mother. His interest in railways is already evident, as his toy train can be seen on the step to their left.

William Nash was 19 years old when this portrait was taken in May 1928.

Nash's photographs themselves offer something new. Many reflect the styles of later years, placing the train firmly in the context of its environment. In so doing they give us a glimpse through a glass, darkly at a world which is long gone.

From Cheltenham in 1926, before he entered the railway industry, we find a photograph of a train on the former Midland & South Western Junction Railway at Charlton Kings. It is a silent image from the platform end of a locomotive type and, indeed, a railway now almost forgotten. But it is an image that serves to remind us of the handsome design of even the most workaday of railway locomotives: a sight making time spent at this outpost well worthwhile.

Another picture, this time of an open-cabbed Great Western 'Metro' tank shunting a couple of horse vans at Radley looks more like a model railway than any reality we know today. Tracks, platforms and grass are all there is to be seen in a view of almost bland tidiness. To modern eyes such a view seems most unlikely. Where is the rubbish and debris we somehow expect to inhabit every scene? The past truly is a foreign country.

Many of Nash's photographs offer new insights for the historian. A train on the Ashover Light Railway, a Sentinel railcar on Jersey (and a view of the Quayside Tramway at Weymouth from the boat that took him there), the Lynton & Barnstaple - all these lines have been photographed before but from Nash we get a new and informal view.

By bringing Nash's photographs into the public arena, Kate Robinson has opened up a treasure trove for the railway historian. At the same time we get a picture of a developing railway career, of the experience gained by undertaking a range of roles at wide-ranging locations and of a young man's desire to explore the world around him. It was to be a career tragically and ironically cut short by the Harrow & Wealdstone disaster in 1952. But these photographs recording a vanished world ensure that memories of William Nash will remain for new generations.

Andrew Scott, Head of National Railway Museum, York

Introduction and Acknowledgements

When, in 2002, Kate and Robert were researching the material for the first compilation of William Nash's pictures called *Cumbrian Railway Photographer*, a large amount of time was spent dating the pictures. This was fascinating detective work, as only a very few of the album entries had dates. Sadly, as both the book and its matching exhibitions were being created that summer, Kate's mother (William's wife) died. In the resulting sort out, a significant amount of further material surfaced. There were only a few new pictures but there was much railway documentation and a notebook in which William had dated and described his photos. Initially his dates were simply the year; later, day and month were added. The early dates in the notebook look to have been done retrospectively.

William who was born at St Bees, Cumbria in January 1909 where his father was a schoolmaster, turns out to have been only 13 when he took his first railway pictures in 1922, a year younger than the date we worked with in *Cumbrian Railway Photographer*.

In the present volume the scope is nationwide. It is the attempt to offer what we consider to be the remaining worthwhile material from the collection. We hope that many of the pictures will be regarded as worthy photographs in their own right. However, some have knowingly been added whose pictorial quality is not the best. Every photographer knows there is an appreciable waste factor in the exercise. William Nash was very young when he started taking railway pictures and that alone justified including some of the 'seconds'. Additionally certain ones are of such rare subjects and situations that they merited consideration.

The full online catalogue can be found at www.forsythe.demon.co.uk/nash.htm

In addition to the sources in the Bibliography, we wish to thank:

To Peter Tatlow for writing the Preface.
To Andrew Scott for writing the Foreword.
To Robert Gratton of Dronfield for help interpreting the Ashover and Leek & Manifold images.
To Alan Marshall who translated some of the Esperanto documents.
To David Postle of the Kidderminster Railway Museum.
To David Präkel, Photoworkshops, Haltwhistle.
To Peter Van Zeller of the Ravenglass & Eskdale Railway.
To Michael Stone for proof reading.
To Rolf Sten for answering questions about Swedish Railways.
To Caroline Wheble, Edgeborough School.
To Tony Money, Archivist, Radley College.
To *Railnews* for printing an appeal for information for details about William's Nash's career and Alan Sutcliffe for responding.
To *Railway Bylines*, *Steam Railway* and *Backtrack* for publishing some selections of pictures and the feedback these engendered.
To the *West Herts Post* for permission to publish extracts from the *West Herts Post and Watford Newsletter*, 16th October, 1952.
And finally to my husband John, and sisters, Mary and Margaret, for their help and encouragement at all times.

Produced by Raphael Tuck & Sons, Ltd., For the Furness Railway
"F.R. Rolling Stock (The Present)"
Series No. 19

POST

The Furness Railway passes throu
English Lake District and along some
most picturesque Coast Scenery in the
Kingdom.

Printed in England

This is one of a
set Mr Mason gave
me for you the other
day. I'm not sure if
you have them, or
not.

13/7/19.   Mum.

W. K. Nash.
Idgeborough.
Guildford.

Chapter One

Railway Photographer at Thirteen: 1922

It seems that Nash's railway interests involved collecting railway postcards prior to conducting railway photography. That is no surprise; the postcard was an indispensable means of communication in his childhood and, during the Edwardian era, it had been adopted by the railway companies as an early collectable that had taken on craze-like dimensions. The Furness Railway (FR) by virtue of his St Bees birth was 'his railway' and thanks to the popularity of Lakeland with visitors, there were already 160 Furness-issued postcards in Nash's childhood. These covered a very diverse range of subjects: posters, steamers, Lakeland views. That trains and locomotives would appeal to the small child is no surprise.

Both front and back of the card opposite have their own message. The card was one of six in an officially-issued set called 'F.R. Rolling Stock (The Present)'. It is a straightforward view of Furness Railway No. 129. This was a larger version of the Pettigrew 'Seagull' class with four engines, Nos. 126-129, appearing in 1900-01 for use on the Whitehaven expresses. Nash's pictures of this class appear in *Cumbrian Railway Photographer*. The card is postally used because on the 13th July, 1919, his mother had sent it to him. Mother wrote: 'This is one of a set [the Furness set Series No. 19 – *authors*] Mr Mason gave me for you the other day. I'm not sure if you have them or not'. What a familiar tale, childhood enthusiasm already leaving parent behind. The card is franked St Bees but the 10-year-old Nash is at the other end of the country.

Edgeborough is a preparatory school near Guildford, still functioning although not in the premises Nash knew. That Nash was at school so far from home is a genuinely tragic tale and one that would directly take him into railway photography.

Nash was born on 11th January, 1909, the only child of William and Ida Nash. William (senior), a schoolmaster of St Bees, died in 1910 and Ida in her new house but without qualifications was in trouble. Their house at St Bees called 'Somerby' is still occupied. 'Somerby' was to remind them of Grantham where William's (senior) father had been the Reverend William Nash of Somerby parish. He had seven offspring, two died before 1900; four of the remaining five have a role to play in this tale. His son William had married Ida; there was a daughter 'Aunt Mabel' who was the cause of the William of this book visiting Jersey (and its railways). There are two more siblings, Philip and Kathleen.

Philip was the younger brother of our Nash's father. He was a distinguished career railwayman. He had been to Radley College (where our William would duly go). He had worked on the Great Northern Railway (1897-1899) and then the East Indian Railway (1899-1915). He returned to Britain in World War I and held a series of key jobs like

Director-General of Transportation for the British Expeditionary Force in 1917 and Inspector-General of Transportation in 1918. Post-war he became Director General of Traffic, Ministry of Transport. When he returned home in the middle of the war, another task he felt responsible for was to assist his sister-in-law Ida. She was now a single parent and never remarried. Philip's role was primarily that of bankrolling the situation and offering some key guidance. It was Philip who paid for William's schooling and very probably Philip who, in the year that Nash successfully entered Radley College (September 1922), bought Nash a camera.

Philip was assisted in his role by the fourth sibling, a sister called Kathleen. Kathleen had been born in 1864 and in 1909 had married Reverend H.W. Boustead who was the vicar of Basingstoke. This information unravels a lot of the photographs. Kathleen it appears, physically took charge of young William for long periods from some time in World War I to enable Ida to try to make a living as a matron. The choice of Edgeborough as a prep school and the presence of so many early pictures taken at Basingstoke is explained. Our William once told his wife that 'he felt like a parcel as a child'. His burgeoning railway enthusiasm may have grown out of a desire to enjoy something reliable when his own life was rather chaotic.

William Nash (*far left*) with friends at Edgeborough in the summer of 1922.

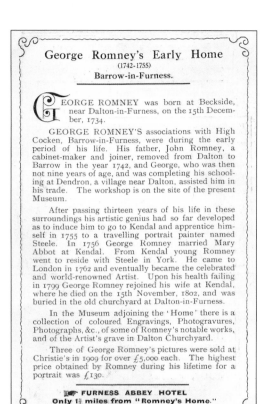

George Romney's Early Home
(1742-1755)
Barrow-in-Furness.

GEORGE ROMNEY was born at Beckside, near Dalton-in-Furness, on the 15th December, 1734.

GEORGE ROMNEY'S associations with High Cocken, Barrow-in-Furness, were during the early period of his life. His father, John Romney, a cabinet-maker and joiner, removed from Dalton to Barrow in the year 1742, and George, who was then not nine years of age, and was completing his schooling at Dendron, a village near Dalton, assisted him in his trade. The workshop is on the site of the present Museum.

After passing thirteen years of his life in these surroundings his artistic genius had so far developed as to induce him to go to Kendal and apprentice himself in 1755 to a travelling portrait painter named Steele. In 1756 George Romney married Mary Abbot at Kendal. From Kendal young Romney went to reside with Steele in York. He came to London in 1762 and eventually became the celebrated and world-renowned Artist. Upon his health failing in 1799 George Romney rejoined his wife at Kendal, where he died on the 15th November, 1802, and was buried in the old churchyard at Dalton-in-Furness.

In the Museum adjoining the 'Home' there is a collection of coloured Engravings, Photogravures, Photographs, &c., of some of Romney's notable works, and of the Artist's grave in Dalton Churchyard.

Three of George Romney's pictures were sold at Christie's in 1909 for over £5,000 each. The highest price obtained by Romney during his lifetime for a portrait was £130.

FURNESS ABBEY HOTEL
Only 1½ miles from "Romney's Home."

Sensitivity to the commercial nature of the railway business might be seen in William's choice of this card, something that would later apply to his career. The Furness Railway had quickly appreciated that it required to be an innovative leader in the tourist business. The card bears the name of Alfred Aslett, the General Manager from 1897. Aslett was the key person who exploited the tourist potential of the Furness and in 1909 (the year of our William's birth), the railway itself bought and restored the house of George Romney the painter, within sight of Barrow's industries. Indeed if patrons strayed too far from the boundaries, they would fall into Hawcoat Quarry.

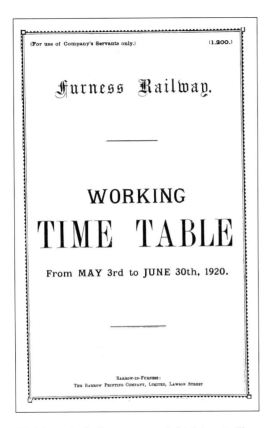

(For use of Company's Servants only.) (1,200.)

Furness Railway.

WORKING

TIME TABLE

From MAY 3rd to JUNE 30th, 1920.

BARROW-IN-FURNESS:
THE BARROW PRINTING COMPANY, LIMITED, LAWSON STREET.

---

6 DOWN.   **WEEK DAYS.**

No. of Train.	65	67	69	71	73	75	77	79	81	84	85
Class of Train.	Goods.	Fast Goods.	Fast Goods.		Engine.	Engine.	Passenger.	Fast Goods.	C Express Goods.		Goods.
No. of Working.	B 11	B5	N.W.		C 8	B 16	C 9	B 15	C 7		C 6
	a.m.	a.m.	a.m.		a.m.	a.m.	a.m.	a.m.	a.m.	a.m.	a.m.
Carnforth {L.&N.W. dep					8 8		8 v 15				
{F. & M.										7 45	8 25
Silverdale							8 24				
Arnside			7 30		8 15		8 31				
Grange {arrive							8 38				
{depart							8 40				
Kents Bank							8 45				
Cark							8 51				B.E.
Plumpton Junction {arr					8 t 0					9 10	
{dep		8 0	8 15		8 25					9 15	
Ulverston {arrive					B.E.		9 4				
{depart							9 7				
Lindal Ore Dep. {arrive		8 20	8 45						9 30	9 w 35	1C 0
{depart			8 r 45								
{Station							9 16				1C 5
Crooklands											
Dalton {arrive							9 19				
{depart							9 20				
Furness Abbey							9 25				
Roose							9 30				
Barrow {Shipyard arrive			9 10								
{Yard											
Hindpool										10 0	
Barrow Central							9 35				
Barrow {Yard depart	8 35						9 10		9 45		
{Central	8 40						9 15 9 v 45		9 55		
Hindpool											
Park {arrive	8 55	9 0					F	F	10 10		
{depart	10 x 0										
Askam {Iron Works							9 25				
{Station {arrive	10 10							9 55			
{depart	10 x 25							F			
Kirkby	11 50										
Foxfield {arrive	11 10						10 5				
{depart	11 50						10 7				
Green Road	12 10										
Millom {arrive	12 20						10 18		10 50		
{depart							10 18	10 30	11 x 0		
Silecroft							10 25				
Bootle							10 35				
Eskmeals							10 42				
Ravenglass							10 47				
Drigg							10 52				
Seascale							10 57				
Sellafield {arrive							11 0				
{depart							11 2	11 30	11 50		
Braystones								x			
Netherton											
St. Bees							11 16				
W'haven {Corkickle {arr							11 x 25	11 50	12 15		
{dep							11 x 27	12 20			
{Preston St. arr											
{Bransty							11 30	12 55			

No.77 Passenger to be worked from Barrow Central by Cx3, and to cross No. 134 Passenger at Corkickle.
No. 1. Engine and Guard to work the 12·20 p.m. Whitehaven to Workington, L.& N.W., and the 1·20 p.m. Workington, L.&N.W., to Whitehaven.
No. 79 Goods to cross No. 134 Passenger at Netnertown.
No. 83 Goods to call where required to attach and at Ulverston to detach Ulverston Cattle on Thursdays, and to call at Lindal Ore Depot when required to detach urgent Goods from beyond Carnforth for Whitehaven and beyond, to go forward by Nos. 91 and 109 Goods.

Nash's trunk of railwayana reveals his interests. The camera and the postcards led him to train photographs as a teenager. The Romney card and a pile of Furness working timetables prompted a career managing the railway? Quite when Nash obtained the working timetables we don't know but he had a remarkably complete set for the FR from 1908 to the Grouping. This page from the 3rd May, 1920 issue shows train services in the Carnforth area that William would become familiar with early in his LMS career.

In turning to Nash's pictures, it is already apparent why certain locations like Cumbria, Basingstoke, Grantham and Radley would feature. Early photography will also reveal a focus on the Stourport and Cheltenham areas. The following four pictures are amongst the first railway pictures Nash ever took back in 1922. An unidentified and apparently un-numbered Dean Goods 0-6-0 shunts at Stourport. Nash gave us little information about the picture but an explanation can be given about why there is the group of Stourport area pictures that follow. Later in this book in Chapter Four some correspondence between Nash and the Lynton & Barnstaple Railway reveals that time was spent during school holidays in the early 1920s at Areley, the settlement on the west bank of the Severn opposite Stourport. Nash did not specify the date any more exactly than 1922, but this group of images seem summery and our view is that the camera entered Nash's life during the summer holiday of 1922 between leaving Edgeborough School and going to Radley College, very possibly as a present from Uncle Philip.

Stourport was to retain its station until 1970 by which time it was worked as part of a curious small triangle of lines: Kidderminster to Bewdley, reverse to Stourport and so back to the main line at nearby Hartlebury. For most of the station's life, between 1862 and 1963, it was served by trains on the Worcester-Shrewsbury Severn Valley line route. One such is seen here headed north hauled by Great Western Railway 'Duke' class No. 3282 *Chepstow Castle*. The coaches are in the all-over chocolate brown or crimson lake liveries that had been used since 1908, the company's famous chocolate and cream livery was officially out of favour between then and 1922. The engine, which had been built in 1899, would stay in traffic until 1937 but not before losing its name in 1930 to a larger 'Castle' class 4-6-0.

From Stourport, the next stop north in the 1920s brought one to the four-way junction at Bewdley, whose station remains lively as part of the present Severn Valley Railway. Nash's focus seems to have been the chance to change there for the six and a half mile run to Cleobury Mortimer on a line heading off into the rural Wyre Forest. Cleobury Mortimer was yet another junction and here Nash stopped for two pictures. He caught another Dean Goods at work with the branch freight. Its number was not recorded but it is not the same engine as seen at Stourport, this one has its cabside number plate, the one at Stourport has not.

The branch line at Cleobury Mortimer ran north around the shoulders of Clee Hill to Ditton Priors. It had been opened in 1908 as an independent Light Railway, which in April 1922 decided to opt for absorption by the Great Western Railway (GWR), which thus took place a few months before the major 1st January, 1923 Grouping. When Nash arrived in 1922 the little line had probably just been taken over and he was fortunate to photograph the Ditton Priors branch train at Cleobury Mortimer looking like an independent operation. *Burwarton*, bought new in 1908 from Manning, Wardle, is in Cleobury Mortimer & Ditton Priors Light Railway colours. It was one of a pair of engines used. Behind it are ex-North London Railway four-wheeled coaches. These did not last long beyond 1926 but a heavily rebuilt *Burwarton* survived until 1954.

Chapter Two

The Year of the Grouping: 1923

The year after his visit to Stourport Nash managed to return to the same area. The upshot was 15 pictures taken from the lineside near Hartlebury by a 14-year-old. His subjects ranged from a '36XX' 2-4-2T (*above*) through examples of the '39XX' inside-cylinder 2-6-2T, various 4-4-0 and 0-6-0 classes, to the 'Aberdare' '26XX' 2-6-0 and the '28XX' 2-8-0. Four are selected for reproduction and although Nash was probably delighted with his bag, doubtless he was a mite miffed that his '39XX' shot was not of the best! The presumption is that the pictures were taken between Hartlebury station and Cutnall Green Halt. Nash's labelling at this period was sketchy and lacks exact dates, engine numbers and train descriptions. The first image is the better of two shots of the '36XX' at work and the train is likely to be a southbound Birmingham to Worcester via Kidderminster working. In identifying the location, the small road running parallel to the railway (*left*) is significant and suggests Nash had gone down the farm access to Valley Farm. There were only 31 of these 2-4-2T designed by Dean for suburban passenger work and current between 1900-1934.

This view at the Hartlebury location looks south. It shows a Dean Goods at the head of one of a procession of freight trains and light engines that passed Nash. This route was a critical artery for the Great Western Railway forming their oldest entry into the Black Country having started life as the Oxford, Worcester & Wolverhampton Railway, which opened through Hartlebury in 1852.

What is likely to be a train of empty private owner coal wagons returning to South Wales for another load was captured storming past Nash's camera from the north. Appropriately the engine is one of the 'Aberdare' class 2-6-0s designed for this sort of work and notable for their outside frames. The train has just surmounted a short climb through Hartlebury and was probably picking up speed as it passed. The summit/change of gradient can be seen in the background and accounts for only the tip of the overbridge being visible.

More or less the same spot and another southbound empty mineral train is stonking along behind a '28XX' class 2-8-0, the Great Western's then modern heavy freight engine. These proved outstandingly successful with 167 built over a long period between 1902-1942. Already in 1924 there were 84 in service. The mineral train is notable for the empty coke wagons, which are identified by the extra height provided by their raves. Coke being lighter than coal the same weight took more space. Once again the gradient change is visible. Another one of Nash's images included the Y shape of the gradient post marking the change immediately south of the Crown Lane overbridge, whose parapets are just visible at the rear of the train in this picture.

Another group of 1923/14-year-old photographs were taken at Oxford Rewley Road LMS station. Every photographer knows that his work involves a lot of wastage and for this schoolboy learning the art not every image could work out. These Oxford images are not of the best but their subject matter justifies the inclusion of two. Acceptable as an image, save for the blackness of an unlit bunker facing the camera, is the first. This shows a London & North Western Railway (LNWR) Whale-designed 'Precursor' class 4-4-2T. These were tank engine versions of a successful 4-4-0 tender engine. Everything about the photograph taken in the first few months of the new London Midland & Scottish Railway says L&NWR (not least the initials on the tank sides). The engine retains its LNWR cast numberplate and, while Nash did not note this number, this is engine No. 562 which became LMS No. 6794. Nash noted that the working was a Bletchley train.

The second image chosen from Oxford is technically rather indifferent. Exactly crisp and the composition with distinctive LNWR corrugated lower quandrant signal, cast-iron sign on lamp and a solo coach (?) would have been fine enough. Nash was probably a bit too excited for this is no solo coach but is an example of what was always a rare breed in the self-contained steam railcar, unlike its ubiquitous diesel successor. The LNWR had built seven of these, which led relatively long lives, the last succumbing in 1948. Rewley Road station was very much an outpost of the LNWR/LMS adjacent to the much more important GWR station. It served trains on a long cross-country route. This led across the main LNWR line at Bletchley and ultimately to Cambridge forming a useful inter-varsity link, which was controversially broken on 1st January, 1968 and about which there continues to be hope of restoration. This will not involve Rewley Road, which was closed to passengers as an economy measure in 1951. The station building survived for decades before preservation and relocation to the Buckinghamshire Railway Centre at Quainton Road. The steam railcars were used to serve some new halts between Oxford and Bicester, which existed between 1905 and 1926, being created when the railcars were introduced. The halts (like Oddington) were ground level and the steps used to access them from the railcar can be made out. Something for the collector to look out for associated with these steam railcars is their appearance on official LNWR postcards. Nash was to revisit this service professionally (*see Chapter Ten*).

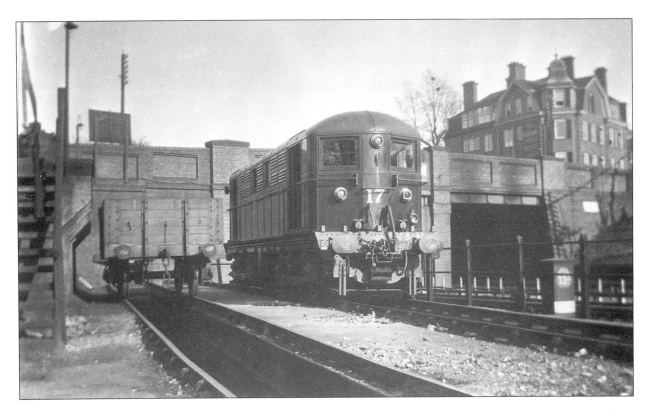

Towards the outset of Nash's railway photography, this teenager was fortunate to visit Harrow and record brand new Metropolitan Railway electric engine No. 17, the last word in new technology. Fortunate because 1923 was the year the Metropolitan was replacing two designs of first generation electric locomotive with this new design. Nash photographed all three (another is shown in the *Cumbrian Railway Photographer*). He took this picture at Harrow where steam engines took over on the run from Baker Street into 'Metroland'. The servicing pit and wagon on the left are for the steam engines. No. 17's sisters had long lives and a couple still exist. No. 17 did not have good fortune, despite being named *Florence Nightingale* in 1927, for a smash in 1943 destroyed it.

Nash's next Metropolitan electric image caught the steeplecab British Westinghouse design of 1905 with No. 7 in Harrow exchange sidings. It could not have remained in use for long after the photo was taken. The Metropolitan Railway was not 'Grouped' in 1923 and remained independent until the London Transport takeover in 1933. It used a variety of steam engines for workings north-west of Harrow, although a couple of years after Nash took his pictures, the traction changeover moved up the line to Rickmansworth from the 5th January, 1925.

Kerr, Stuart had built these Metropolitan class 'H' 4-4-4T in 1920 and so their frequent appearance at Harrow was in a quite restricted time envelope of 1920-25. This image shows No. 109 with a passenger train from Baker Street. Their unusual wheel arrangement suited duties which had little scope for turning, required a fair turn of speed but were not of excessive duration. Two types of passenger stock are featured in this view. Behind the steam engine is the so-called 'Dreadnought' compartment stock. In many respects these were typical of main line non-corridor coaches of the period. Some were built as late as 1923 and many stayed in service until 1961. The front bogie of this coach carries electric pick-up shoegear which was to assist the overall power supply when coupled to the electric locomotive. The later locomotives (*see page 23*) and these coaches became the subject of a hugely popular Hornby 'O' gauge model. To the left of the picture is one of the electric-multiple-unit trains whose sliding doors are distinctive. The train shown is thought to be one of the 1921 build.

One of the images dated by Nash as 1923 is the first of what would be several photographs of the Midland & South Western Junction Railway (M&SWJR). This prior to its takeover on the 1st July, 1923 by the Great Western Railway had been a thorn running through the heartland of the larger company. It linked the Midland Railway at Cheltenham with the London & South Western Railway (LSWR) at Andover having had the cheek to use some miles of the Great Western's line east out of Cheltenham past Charlton Kings before gaining its own tracks at (confusingly named) Andoversford. Thereon it ploughed through GWR lands with duplicated stations in towns like Cirencester, Swindon (!) and Marlborough. Nash having family connections, which took him to both Cheltenham and Basingstoke, as this album will further reveal, had excellent reason to use the M&SWJR. Its engines looked wholly different to the GWR or the LSWR, although the GWR worked after takeover to change that. Nash meantime had got his camera to work. This first image

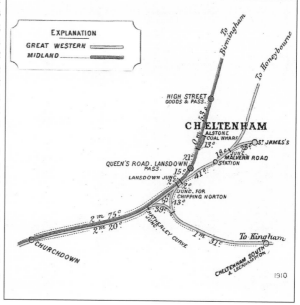

(*left*) was noted by Nash as of M&SWJR engine No. 31 on a Southampton train near Cheltenham. The exact location is something of a surmise but it is likely to be the double-track section of the GWR that M&SWJR trains used between Cheltenham and Andoversford. The train is on an embankment on a left-hand curve pulling uphill and so it is quite possible that this is the first mile or so out from Lansdown Junction at Cheltenham before Cheltenham South and Leckhampton station. Around OS reference SO929208 is our hunch, which would make the buildings to the left Green Farm and thus an area which is wholly built over and unrecognisable today.

The M&SWJR's engineer Tyrell had been responsible for nine 4-4-0 engines built between 1905 and 1914. No. 31 was one which had been built in June 1914 and which was Great Westernised with a Swindon taper boiler in October 1924. Nash caught her in those fleeting months of change around the takeover and whether by accident or design this teenager moved his image into the realm of art. This is not just a record shot, Nash has stopped the moving train but with scudding clouds, the plume of steam and smoke and the hint of winter in the bare bramble to the right and the trees of the skyline left, the image is lifted into realms of impressionism.

Chapter Three

At Radley College: 1924

William Nash arrived at Radley College in September 1922. He was already taking railway pictures. He would take many more whilst at Radley College. In 1924 a run of three choice years for William's railway photography commenced. With access to the school darkroom his subjects could include the railway at Radley itself. These years would also see him travel widely in pursuit of some narrow gauge operations (*see next chapter*).

Radley station was an ideal location for a budding railway photographer. It had opened in 1873, replacing Abingdon Jn, opened in 1856, although the railway had arrived *en route* to Oxford in 1844. Radley was the junction station for Abingdon so the frequent variety of trains ranged from branch line services and Great Western expresses to through traffic from beyond the GWR heading North-South.

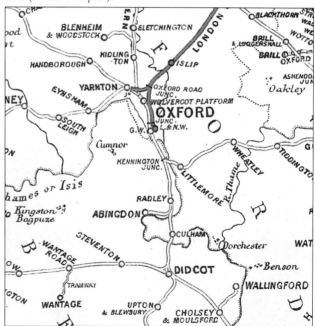

Calling at Radley working towards Oxford is GWR No. 2225 sometime in 1924 (*opposite*). This attractive tank engine is a so-called 'County' class tank 4-4-2T, being the 30-strong tank engine class version of a popular GWR 4-4-0 design. Behind it, the coaches appear to be in the chocolate brown or crimson lake liveries that had temporarily supplanted the favourite GWR chocolate and cream between 1908-1922.

Although what Nash was doing as a teenager was unusual and noteworthy, he was not the first teenage railway photographer. Co-incidentally Radley station a decade before had been host to another 14-year-old taking a series of railway photographs that have survived. This was one Bill Kenning whose work was published in the early 1970s and who had also attended Radley College.

Nash caught GWR No. 1443 shunting horse boxes off the Abingdon branch train during 1924. This was representative of an ubiquitous class of branch engine with a currency between 1868 and 1945. These GWR '517' class 0-4-2Ts were distinctive in later life for their open cabs. Nash never photographed the more modern '14XX' class Collett-designed replacements, several of which still exist, unlike the '517' class. No. 1443 was already an old hand and dated back to 1878. These engines went through all sort of changes in their career. The state Nash found No. 1443 in accords well with another 1920s image of sister engine No. 1440 in J.H. Russell's study of GWR engines. The shared features are the outside bearings on the trailing wheels, vertical-backed bunker and the Belpaire firebox.

The previous chapter found Nash photographing one of the 31 strong '36XX' class at Hartlebury. The West Midlands or the Thames Valley suburbans were their favoured area so it was not surprising that Nash could photograph No. 3630 in 1924 passing Radley station bound for Oxford. The coaches were starting to seem antique by the mid-1920s although there were plenty in traffic like this. They dated from the William Dean era on the Great Western (1890-1905). Front and back are two 40 ft full luggage and brake vans. These are sandwiching the distinctive Dean clerestory stock. None seem to be in the chocolate and cream livery. Radley station is still open but the branch to Abingdon lost its passenger service to Beeching in 1963. The presence of the MG factory kept freight trains running for some years after.

Fourteen-year-old boys can be foolhardy and this would seem the case for what pictorially is one of the best Radley images showing a Churchward Mogul 2-6-0 bowling along with coal trucks.

Nash's Cheltenham links ensured he was photographing around the town in 1924 although most of our selection will focus on 1926. This 1924 image is of GWR 4-4-0 *City of Bath* hauling a Wolverhampton to Penzance express. The 20 'Cities' had quite short lives between 1903 and 1931 but will always be associated with the fame that *City of Truro* gained in 1904 when a speed of 102 mph was claimed. *City of Bath* herself was familiar to a 1920s schoolboy by being the subject of a contemporary Bassett-Lowke model.

Whilst associated with Cheltenham, his focus was on this house. This was Rylstone, Montpellier Parade, Cheltenham. It seems that this property was probably obtained by Uncle Philip Nash for Ida Nash, William's mother, to run as a rest home called The Imperial Nursing Home. This would remain Nash's mother's home address until early in 1932 when her business failed. She was then obliged to look to her son for help and would live with him until she died.

In defining this location more exactly, Nash's pictures leave several clues. The presence of houses in the background and some open space on the right in the photos labelled for southbound trains are one clue. Another is that the trains featured are both of LMS and GWR ownership. This suggests it must be the main line south-west of Lansdown Junction north of which the two railways split. The route north beyond Lansdown station, which remains the main line today, in Nash's time, was purely for LMS trains. That is confirmed by Nash's description on this picture as 'London Express' which, since its motive power is Great Western 'Metro' 2-4-0T No. 1464, defines the train as originating in Cheltenham's St James station. The trackage which both companies used south-west of Lansdown station was very busy. So much so that on the 9th August, 1942 a quadrupled length of track between Lansdown Junction and Gloucester was completed. This reverted to double track in 1966/67. This location we conclude is Ordnance Survey reference SO 926316 facing towards the town of Cheltenham. This makes the houses on the left the back prospect of Granley Road.

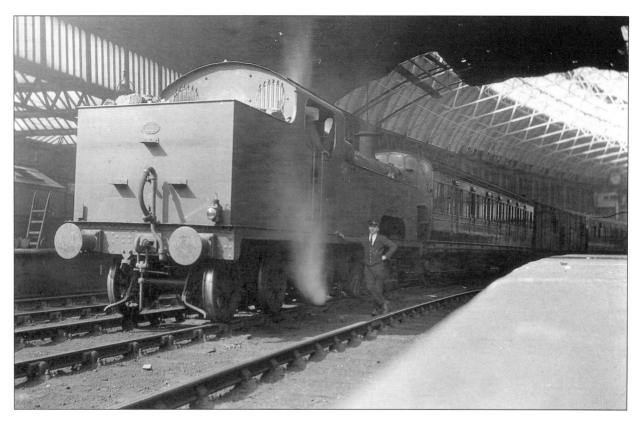

The last of the 1924 images chosen sees Nash at Birmingham New Street. It is the only picture he took there. Both the Victorian era station and its 1960s rebuild were appallingly dark. Nash's picture shows an ex-Midland Railway 0-6-4T, a so-called 'Flatiron'. The engine is coupled to a coach and then two horseboxes and another coach. Nash had persuaded a railwayman to pose and the manner in which steam is lingering reveals the slow shutter speed Nash must have used to gain this picture.

Chapter Four

From Basingstoke to the East Midlands: 1925

Family connections gave Nash access to Basingstoke station, which led to a series of 1925 images. Three large groups of 4-6-0 engines sharing a general outline dominated main line expresses in the mid-1920s through the station. These classes 'H15', 'N15' and 'S15' went back to 1914 and the Urie era on the London & South Western Railway. The Southern Railway would continue to build examples until 1936 and they would remain in service well into the 1960s. Engine 523 was handling a down Southampton express when photographed by Nash on a wet day. This 'H15' had been new in September 1924; the pristine nature of the front end suggests she is barely run in. In the second part of the 1920s, problems with drifting smoke saw the fitting of smoke deflectors. This changed the appearance considerably.

This Basingstoke photograph is of sister engine SR 'H15' class No. 522, likewise nearly new. The train was bound for Bournemouth. From one aspect this is a detailed view of a locomotive tender, from another it is a picture expressing all the anticipation of a journey ahead to the holiday lands of the South-West. If the angle seems familiar this is because in 1924 a commercial photographer took a picture in like vein from a platform end at Waterloo. This became the basis of a very famous Southern Railway poster with a little boy looking up to the engine driver in his cab. The engine in both poster and Nash image came from the same Urie 4-6-0 mould. The Urie 4-6-0 philosophy gained its success in simplicity, with two large outside cylinders and a high running plate for ease of maintenance.

Nash caught up with Southern No. 447 during 1925 on a wet day at Andover Junction. This engine had been built by the London & South Western's Eastleigh works in 1910 as a member of that company's 10-strong 'T14' class, the first 4-6-0s built specifically for the Bournemouth run. The engine was to run into the early British Railways period but along the way it saw a lot of changes. Its original designer, Dugald Drummond, had built it without superheating and with an unusual firebox water tube system. After Urie's arrival on the LSWR he removed the water tube firebox and fitted superheating with an extended smokebox, which is the state in which Nash saw No. 447. Later rebuilding removed the splashers and substituted a high running plate. It was the vast bulk of the splashers, which gained the class their 'paddlebox' nickname. Compare the engine with the previous 'H15' pictures and it is clear how difficult accessing the motion would be. Not so obvious is that the design is a complicated four-cylinder engine.

In transition from the South to the East Midlands it is not inappropriate to visit Banbury. This Nash 1925 image appears as his only one from that town. Banbury was a major junction of the GWR, LNWR and GCR whose one route led north-east. This branch, by then the London & North Eastern Railway's (LNER), enabled a connection to the ex-Great Central main line. The key point of this linkage was to transfer trains from the North and East avoiding London and running to destinations in the South and West. Nash did not identify the working but it is likely to be one of these inter-company cross-country trains, which is probably changing engines at Banbury. The engine is LNER No. 5262, which had been Great Central No. 262, a Robinson design Atlantic 4-4-2 of 1906. The year of this view was also the year the engine was fitted with a superheated boiler. The engine lasted until February 1948.

During 1925 Nash made excursions to three significant East Midland railway centres: Grantham, Nottingham and Lincoln. Grantham was a staging post on the East Coast Main Line and a junction for Nottingham and Lincolnshire. Many of the main line trains changed their engines here. The locomotive shed on the west side of the station was a focal point of activity. It was a clear attraction for Nash's lens. Engines visible in this scene include former Great Northern 4-4-0 and 4-4-2 types. With the coming of the diesel, Grantham lost much of this importance and the shed, which had stabled 41 locomotives in 1959, was closed in 1963. The parish of Somerby at Grantham was where Nash's grandfather had been rector.

In 1925 the Gresley Pacifics, to be immortalised by *Flying Scotsman*, were new machines and shared much of the main line work with the Ivatt Atlantic engines, the preceding generation of Great Northern, now London & North Eastern Railway, express engine. Nash evidently went to Grantham to see both types at close quarters. He came away with six pictures of the Ivatt Atlantic 4-4-2s. Ivatt Atlantic No. 4407 has stopped at Grantham on a southbound express. Details to enjoy include the station lamp with name and the water column. Just like the stagecoach horses of old, the steam engine required regular watering and Grantham was a steam age staging post. The large 6 ft 8 in. diameter driving wheels are very clear. No. 4407 had been Great Northern No. 1407 and would have been less than 20 years old when Nash photographed her.

What an exciting scene at the platform end of Grantham station as a northbound express steams through. Atlantic No. 4454 double-heads another class member with a Leeds-bound express. Nash had a good eye for composition and used the venerable six-wheeled coach (*right*) and the warehouse (*left*) to push the eyes to the oncoming train. To have set all this up and stopped the moving train for a 16-year-old photographer in 1925 was quite a feat.

The undoubted highlight of the visit must have been the chance to photograph the Gresley Pacific 4-6-2 engines. Here in a servicing siding at the south end of the station No. 4475 *Flying Fox* takes on water and her crew are content to pose for the young photographer. This was the sixth engine in this famous class and would have been about two years old when Nash saw her. The engines were later rebuilt considerably but this photograph records No. 4475 in its original 'A1' condition. The appearance of the locomotive number on the tender and not the cabside is a feature of early LNER livery.

At the north end of Grantham station Nash photographed No. 4480 running in with a southbound train. The engine would later on be named *Enterprise* (there is no plate above the wheel splashers). The engine was another of the 10 'A1s' delivered, like No. 4475, in 1923 with many more built in 1924/25 as Nash was out there taking his photographs. Several detail changes would follow, notches would appear on the bufferbeam and the boiler mountings would be reduced in height. The notches arose from one of the early class members arguing with the curved platforms at Newcastle. In 1927 Gresley fitted an improved boiler to this engine to increase her tractive effort by 22 per cent and thereby become the first class 'A3' engine. Other details like the milk churns and classic Great Northern Railway centrally-pivoted somersault signals on their lattice metal posts help set the scene.

The LNER had a branch from Grantham to Nottingham (ex-Great Northern) and it was also present in the form of the ex-Great Central Railway main line from Sheffield to London. Nonetheless Nottingham Midland station was the heart of Nottingham's railways and the only station to survive in operation today. Nash took a sequence of photographs there; in this case LMS No. 2024 poses standing alone in a centre road. To have no doubts that this is Nottingham look at the names on the buildings to the left. No. 2024 would have appeared as a mammoth tank engine, sufficiently iconic of modern railways before World War I for the German train manufacturer Märklin to have modelled the class. Despite their powerful appearance, the engines were not the most effective. They were nicknamed 'Flatirons' and were in existence between 1907-1938. The extended smokebox indicates that the engine had recently been superheated and reboilered. The lining on the livery can be made out and the engine would have been in a rich crimson lake livery, which was changed to black after 1928.

In 1925 LMS engine No. 1048 would have been about a year old. Its LMS maker's plate is legible on the front splasher. Nash noted that it was handling a London express at Nottingham. Shining in crimson lake it would have been an attractive sight and the image gains interest from the miniature semaphore signals the Midland Railway employed for shunting movements, in the foreground. The class that No. 1048 came from originated with Midland Railway No. 1000 (preserved by the National Railway Museum) in 1901. This so-called Midland Compound was that company's most powerful passenger locomotive design. The Compound term described the manner in which the steam was used twice in first the inside high- and then outside low-pressure cylinders.

The most common Midland Railway passenger engines were a host of inside-cylindered 4-4-0s built from 1876 and whose much altered design was continued by the LMS for new build as its '2P' class. Nash captured one of these double-heading one of the larger Midland Compounds at Nottingham. Engine No. 396 fronts No. 1037. The former went back to 1891 but had been considerably altered in its life and had just recently had another rebuild to the '483' class specification in 1923.

For many enthusiasts, the apex of Victorian locomotive design came in the single-wheeled express engine: single-wheeled as in one enormous driving wheel for speed. When Nash started taking pictures, there were few survivors but he caught this former Midland Railway example, No. 655, in Nottingham station in 1925, the very year it was withdrawn. MR on the bufferbeam indicates that it retained Midland Railway livery. These engines were known as the Midland 'Spinners' and spent their entire lives in crimson lake colours. There had once been 85 of these engines built from 1887, 43 of them made it into LMS hands in 1922, the last survivor going in 1928. Their fame ensured that, even back in the 1920s, the final engine in service was retained for preservation. Nowadays it is part of the National Railway Museum collection.

Nash's 1925 visit to Nottingham had scored the key Midland Railway passenger engine designs. He concluded his selection with one of the real antiques. This was a former Midland Railway '1' class engine with a 2-4-0 wheel arrangement, '1' because the class leader had once been Midland No. 1. Renumbered as No. 149 in 1907, Nash's subject had been Midland No. 10 when new. It had gained the LMS crimson lake livery but was definitely an old stager dating from 1876. Incredibly some of the class were rebuilt after this photograph was taken and the last survived until 1950.

Lincoln has been a railway centre since 1846. Four railway companies and two important stations arrived on the flat land beneath the cathedral. Three of the companies and one of the two stations joined the LNER in 1923 and just over 60 years later the erstwhile Midland Railway Lincoln St Marks station was closed in a sensible piece of rationalisation. For Nash the appeal in 1925 lay in the possibility of photographing engines from four of the LNER's constituents. Representing the former North Eastern Railway was one of their large express engines, a Worsdell Atlantic 4-4-2 No. 1792. There were 20 class members operational between 1903-1948.

All Nash's Lincoln pictures were taken at the surviving Central station. The two engines in this picture are both 4-4-0 types. No. 106c was a one-time Great Central Railway engine. In the background is a Great Eastern Railway example from LNER 'D13' or the 'Humpty Dumpty' class. It seems that the background engine was still in Great Eastern colours whilst No. 106c has LNER lettering but retains the GCR numberplate on the engine. The number, 106c, (c for Central) is an interim measure. It is a member of the LNER 'D9' class. Younger readers may be confused about the fact that Central was built by the Great Northern Railway and not the Great Central. Despite that, a Great Central engine is present and that company had two routes into the city from the west and one from the north-east.

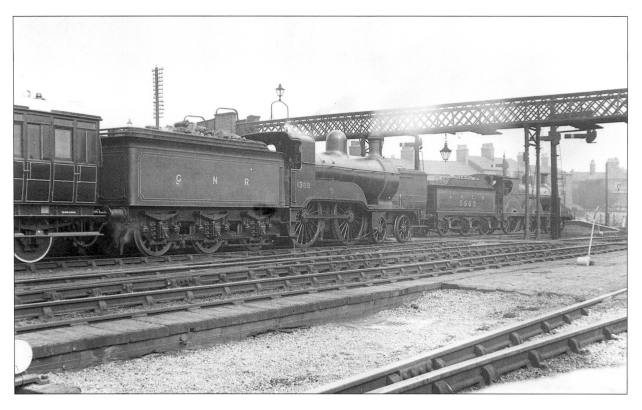

Presumably only a little later and the same vantage point offered another two examples of LNER 4-4-0. In their shades of green and with teak coaches (see how the one on the left gleams), these machines were a magnificent sight. This time the ex-Great Central engine has its full LNER No. 5563 and is an older beast, classed 'D7' by the LNER. It dates back to the late 1880s. Nearer the camera engine No. 1369 retained its full Great Northern Railway livery.

A magnificent example of the former Great Eastern Railway 'Claud Hamilton' class 4-4-0 is the subject of this portrait. No. 8824 is absolutely gleaming in LNER apple green, even in black and white. The engine was built in 1909 and withdrawn in 1957. The extensive lining out, even on wheel spokes, is evident as is the brass chimney rim. The Great Eastern engines came to Lincoln by virtue of a long joint line with the Great Northern Railway, which ran from March in Cambridgeshire to Doncaster. The 'Claud Hamiltons' changed shape somewhat in their lives. No. 8824 in this picture represents a mid stage known as LNER class 'D15'.

Nash took one picture at Lincoln of the humble British 0-6-0 goods engine, a genre that was numbered in tens of thousands. Nash's compositional skill makes this into art with his stress on the equally humble ground signal in the foreground for shunting movements, and the water crane and its associated paraphernalia. A scene of the everyday hardware to compare with the glitterati in the previous images. Engine No. 3073 had come from the Great Northern Railway (see how the cab outline resembled the ex-GNR 4-4-0 No. 1369) but by 1925 was in somewhat work-stained LNER livery.

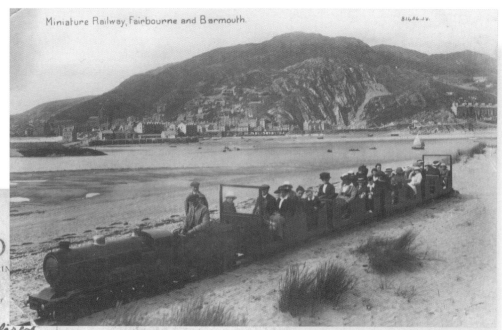

Miniature Railway, Fairbourne and Barmouth.

81486 JV.

I'm sure this will interest
you. I got it yesterday at
Barmouth, tho' I didn't see
the little train. We had a
lovely day, motoring through
Dolgelly to Barmouth, tho' we
had to come back the same
way, unforch. A most gorgeous
afternoon revering, + then today
thick black clouds + pouring rain
again! Mum. May 29/26.

W. K. Nash.
Edgeborough.
Guildford.

56

Chapter Five

Narrow Gauge Railway Visits

Nash would have been six when the Ravenglass & Eskdale Railway (R&ER) started its transformation to the miniature 15 in. gauge. As he spent at least some time at nearby St Bees, it was evidently going to impact on him. Additionally it is clear that other narrow gauge systems were entering his psyche some time before he obtained his camera. Various systems appear in his postcard albums and two relevant postcards come from the Fairbourne Railway in North Wales. The first was posted by Nash's mother Ida, on holiday in the Barmouth area on 29th May, 1920 (*opposite*), to William at his prep school.

The Fairbourne Railway had been created at the same time in 1915/16 as the Ravenglass & Eskdale had been transformed and by the same team of Bassett-Lowke and allies in the guise of Narrow Gauge Railways Ltd. In its case it was a moribund 2 ft gauge horse tramway. The interest for Nash was obvious and his mother appreciated this in 1920. Her 1920 visit would appear to have been followed up by a family visit in 1921 during which William was recorded by a Barmouth portrait photographer.

Nash's railway photography started in 1922. From 1923, the Ravenglass & Eskdale Railway joined his early subjects. His fascination with the narrow gauge continued and this chapter visits the five systems that Nash did. *Cumbrian Railway Photographer* contained many of the Ravenglass images, more of these now follow. The essential appealing feature of the line, beyond its local location for Nash, was that the father of British model railways, one Wenman Bassett-Lowke, had revived the line in the middle of World War I. This was done by changing a moribund 3 ft gauge iron ore mineral railway into a miniature railway.

The second card shown from Nash's collection is not postally used and we might think he collected it. It is a Bassett-Lowke produced card which is known to use a Bassett-Lowke print from late 1916, the first season of the 15 in. Fairbourne Railway. The train is lettered for Narrow Gauge Railways and the engine is an 'Improved Little Giant' 4-4-2 *Prince Edward of Wales*. The engine worked at Fairbourne until 1923 and remains in existence.

Outside Ravenglass shed in the summer of 1924 Nash found *Colossus*. This engine had started life on the private Staughton Manor Railway as *John Anthony* in 1913 but came to Ravenglass in 1916 when it was renamed. When purchased, its owner, Captain Howey, was a prisoner of war. He later came to fame by promoting the other great 15 in. gauge railway, the Romney, Hythe & Dymchurch. *Colossus* was used on the R&ER until 1927 being too much of a scale model for a lengthy career.

Another August 1924 picture, and probably from the same visit, shows the other scale model Pacific engine that the railway was then operating. It is near Ravenglass station with the standard gauge exchange sidings behind. The engine is named *Sir Aubrey Brocklebank*, after the Cunard magnate who lived near the 'Ratty' and who acted as a patron between 1917-1929. The engine was the only new steam engine bought by Narrow Gauge Railways during their ownership of the R&ER and its maker, Hunts of Bournemouth, built no other steam engines. New in 1919, it worked for less than a decade before being rebuilt none too successfully into the articulated and first *River Mite*.

Nash identified this train as the 12.30 pm preparing to leave Ravenglass. *Colossus* is coupled on and it looks as if *Sans Pareil* is just backing on prior to double-heading in the last of this group. *Sans Pareil*, which had been on the line since 1915, looks well worn. She was a Bassett-Lowke Atlantic which was really too small for the work. There were three groups of these so-called 'Little Giant' 4-4-2s. *Sans Pareil* (without parallel) came from the final group of three and, unlike her two surviving sisters, life at Ravenglass saw her condemned in 1926.

Whereas the Ravenglass station site remained in one place, the upper terminal of the 15 in. gauge was a fluid affair between 1915-1926. In the four years before 1926, when Nash was evidently deeply interested in the line, the terminal was beside the former miner's cottages at Dalegarth. This August 1924 image shows *Sir Aubrey Brocklebank* facing downhill at the Dalegarth terminus. A turntable had been put in at Dalegarth in 1922. The train has a covered coach, which is a Heywood-style bogie saloon coach. The other vehicles are Bassett-Lowke-style four-wheelers and an open Heywood truck behind the tender.

Ravenglass & Eskdale Railway.

======

WORKING TIME TABLE,

SEPT. 22nd, 1924,
Until Further Notice.

In the summer the revived Ravenglass & Eskdale needed helpers and a crew of students and youngsters helped out. William Nash was one and he probably became familiar with a wooden bungalow that was erected around 1922 as temporary staff accommodation at Ravenglass station. The exact detail of his commitment is not known but it seems to foreshadow his interest in standard gauge railway operating. His railwayana chest contains a 1924 printed working timetable from the Ravenglass & Eskdale Railway (*left*).

Rather more extraordinary is this manuscript working timetable (*opposite*) for the Ravenglass line produced in Nash's own hand. By 1928 he was working for the LMS around the Carnforth area and its production probably did not tax him unduly but it remains a wonderful survival, the more so in coming from a period when an intensive stone traffic was being worked as well. Between 1928-1930, the stone traffic between the crusher and Ravenglass was being worked in some specially built bogie hopper trucks and Working Number R2 should be this traffic. After 1930, the traffic from Murthwaite was handled by standard gauge trains. The presence of one return mixed train running the length of the line is evidence that the line still functioned actively as a common carrier handling general goods: although the limited extent of such traffic in summer was such that there was no dedicated goods train.

Ravenglass and Eskdale Railway. Working Time-Table from July 9th till September 23rd, 1923.

Down. — Week Days. — Sundays.

Train Number.	1	3	5	7	9	11	13	15	17	19	21	23	25	27	29	31	33	35	37	39	41	43	45	47	1	3	5	7
Class of Train.	Mixed	Light Engine	Pass	Stone	Pass	Stone	Pass	Stone	Pass	Pass	Pass	Pass	Pass	Stone	Pass	Pass	Pass	Stone	Stone	Pass	Pass	Pass			Pass	Pass	Pass	Pass
Working Number.	Ra1	R1		R1		R2	Ra1	R2	Ra2	Ra1	R1	R1	Ra2	R2	Ra3	Ra3	R1	R2	Ra2	Ra2	Ra3				Ra1	R1	Ra1	R1
			RThO		RTh								FO	FS		S	F5O	FS	S	S	80							
	a.m	a.m	a.m	a.m	a.m	a.m	a.m	a.m					p.m		p.m	p.m	p.m	p.m	p.m	p.m	p.m				a.m	a.m	p.m	p.m
Ravenglass. d	7.20	7.45	8.20		8.35	9.5	9.35		11.0	11.20	11.40		1.50	2.0	2.55	3.15			4.0	4.20	6.25	6.50			10.0	10.50	2.30	5.55
Murthwaite Crusher. d			8.35		8.45	9.10			11.14					2.14					4.14									
" Loop. a / d		7.59			9x0																							
" " d				8.55			10.55			p.m	1.35	1.46			x	4.0												6.15
Irton Road. d	7.46		8x45		9.10		9x56			11x41	1x1		2.10		2x13	3x16	3.36			4.41	6.46	7.11			10.21	11.11	2.51	6x23
Eskdale Green. a / d	7.46		8.53		9.15		10x1			11.46	1.6		2.1	2x7	2.18		3.21	3.41			4.46	6.51	7.16			10.26	11x16	2.56	6.28
Quarry. a				9.14			x	11.14					1.54	2.15				4.19										
Beckfoot. a	Q		Q		Q		Q							Q							Q	7.6	Q					Q
" " d																						7.10						
Dalegarth. a	8.3		9.10		9.32		10.18			12.3	1.23		2.35		3.33	3.50				5.3	7.15	7.33			10.41	11.33	3.13	6.45

Up.

Train Number.	2	4	6	8	10	12	14	16	18	20	22	24	26	28	30	32	34	36	38	40	42	44	46	48	2	4	6	8
Class of Train.	Pass	Stone	Pass	Stone	Pass	Stone	Stone	Light Engine	Pass	Pass	Stone	Stone	Stone	Pass	Pass	Stone	Stone	Pass	Mixed	Light Engine	Pass	Pass			Pass	Pass	Pass	Pass
Working Number.	Ra1	R2		R1		Ra1	R2	R1		R1	R1	Ra2	Ra1		R1	R1	Ra3	Ra2	Ra1	R1	Ra3				Ra1	R1	Ra1	R1
			RThO		RTh				SO			FS	FQ	FO	FS	F5O	FS	S	S		S	SO						
	a.m	a.m	a.m	a.m	a.m	a.m	a.m	a.m	a.m	a.m	a.m	p.m	p.m	p.m	p.m	p.m	p.m	p.m	p.m	p.m	p.m	p.m			a.m	p.m	p.m	p.m
Dalegarth. d	8.20		9.30		9.55	11.20			12.40	1.55				2.55	3.0			5.13	5.20		7.20	8.24			11.0	1.25	6.5	7.10
Beckfoot. a	8.24		9.34		9.59				Q		Q				Q				Q		Q	Q			Q	Q	Q	Q
" " d	8.32		9.39		10.5	Q			Q												7.25							
Quarry. a		8.40		10x13	10.8		12.0					2.45	2.55			5.0					7.25							
" " d		8.57																					11.9					
Eskdale Green. a	8.40		9.47	10x2	10.20	11.30			12.50	2.25				3.5	3.10			5.20	5.30		7.35	8.30	11x16	1.35	6.15	7.20		
Irton Road. d			9.52		11.35				12.55						3.10								11.22	1.41	6x21	7.26		
" " d	8x46		10x0		10.26	11x41			1.1	2x11				3.4	3.16	3.16		5.26	5.36		7.41	8.36						
Murthwaite Loop. a					10.15				12.19						3.14		3.25	5.19			X							
" " d									12.55								3x28				5.44							
" Crusher. " d		X	10.0			12.0			p.m			2.55		3.10				5.0										
Ravenglass. " a	8.4	9.4	10.14	10.18		10.44	11.59	12.14		1.6	1.19	2.29	3.9		3.24	3.34	3.40	5.14		5.44	5.54	6.0	7.59	8.54	11.40	1.59	6.39	7.44

All down trains to stop at Muncaster when required to take up; and all up trains when required to set down.

F. Except Fridays.
FO. Fridays Only.
FS. Except Fridays and Saturdays.
F5O. Fridays and Saturdays only.
Q. Stops if required.
R. Runs if required.
S. Except Saturdays.
SO. Saturday only.
Th. Except Thursdays.
ThO. Thursdays only.
X. Cross.
Y. Cross on Saturdays.
Z. Cross except on Fridays and Saturdays.

63

Another popular narrow gauge line with the summer tourists was not going to have the happy history that the Ravenglass has had. The Ravenglass was closed before Bassett-Lowke arrived and had a tricky time again around 1960. In Devon the 2 ft gauge Lynton & Barnstaple Railway (L&BR) had linked the two towns since 1898. Like other minor lines that Nash knew, his first encounters took place just at the period when most of these operations were taken into the large 1923-grouped companies, the 'Big Four'. The L&BR was taken into the Southern and although matters initially looked rosy, closure and dismantling followed in 1935.

Before Nash reached the railway in 1924 he had been writing to its manager Mr Drewett in 1921/22 (the three letters from Drewett are reproduced). Whilst Nash was at prep-school near Basingstoke, his widowed mother was struggling to make a living. Nash was packed off to various locations in his holidays and the addresses to which Drewett wrote (see the letter bottoms) become significant in explaining some of Nash's other pictures (consider the Stourport/Hartlebury group reproduced in Chapter One).

Lynton & Barnstaple Railway.

TELEGRAMS
DREWETT, RAILWAY,
BARNSTAPLE.

C. E. DREWETT,
SECRETARY & MANAGER.

Please quote No. 4/2708

PILTON BRIDGE,

In reply to your

BARNSTAPLE.

Dec.13th 21.

Dear Sir,

In reply to yours of the 10th inst. The whole of this Company's stock is fitted with the Vacuum Automatic Brake.

The safety loading gauge measurements are from rail level, height at side 8'6", at centre 9'6", width 6'4". The height from the rail to truck floor level is 2 feet.

Yours truly,

C Drewett

Mr W.K.Nash,

The Lion Hotel,

GUILDFORD.

B. L.

Lynton & Barnstaple Railway.

TELEGRAMS
DREWETT, RAILWAY,
BARNSTAPLE.

Please quote No. 4/2708

In reply to your

C. E. DREWETT,
SECRETARY & MANAGER.

PILTON BRIDGE,

BARNSTAPLE.

Jan.5th 22.

Dear Sir,

    In reply to yours of the 2nd inst.
All stations have double lines for crossing purposes.
The electrical tablet is in use & the sections are
Barnstaple Town Station - Pilton Yard(Barnstaple
Depot)-Chelfham-Bratton-Blackmoor - Woody Bay -
Lynton Stations.

        Yours truly,

        Drewett

Mr W.K.Nash,
  Areley House,
    Private Hotel,
      Stourport,
        Worcs.

        T. P.

Lynton & Barnstaple Railway.

Nº4/2708

TELEGRAMS,
DREWETT, RAILWAY,
BARNSTAPLE.

MANAGER'S OFFICE,
Pilton Bridge,
Barnstaple,
Jan.11th 1922

Dear Sir,

    In reply to yours of the 8th inst.   There are three
Passenger Halts on this line viz. Snapper between Barnstaple,Pilton
Yard & Chelfham; Parracombe between Blackmoor & Woody Bay;
Caffyns between Woody Bay & Lynton.   There is no loop for the
passing of trains at these Halts.   There is no stopping place at
Rowley.   The distances from Barnstaple Town are as shewn under.

Barnstaple Town to:-

	Miles	Chains
Barnstaple Goods (Pilton Yd.)		34
Snapper	2.	55.
Chelfham	4.	54.
Bratton	7.	55.
Blackmoor	11.	64.
Parracombe	14.	34
Woody Bay	16.	0.
Caffyns	17.	32.
Lynton	19	25.

Mr W.K.Nash,
  Areley House,
    Stourport,
      Worcs.

      Yours truly,

      C. Drewett   H.

Nash's visit took place during his Easter holidays in April 1924 (the vegetation is not in leaf). It seems likely that his earlier correspondence with the then independent company had paved the way to gain access to the line's workshops at Pilton, Barnstaple, despite the line having become part of the Southern Railway on 1st January, 1923. Mr Drewett who had managed the railway for 22 years had retired with the take-over. Since he continued to live in Barnstaple, he was possibly involved in the teenager's visit. The engine Nash photographed at Pilton was *Lyn*, a 2-4-2T of 1898. Save for the recent appearance of a stovepipe chimney, she was still in her genuine L&BR state and this engine has always attracted interest because she was a one-off import from the Baldwin Locomotive Works in the USA.

Later, *Lyn* was seen taking a Lynton-bound train past Pilton works. The train is in L&BR colours and the L&BR lettering can be made out on the front bogie van. This is one of the two 1897 bogie goods brake vans, either No. 5 or 14. The coaches behind are in two liveries. The rear coach is in the usual L&BR red brown and varnished white. Right at the end of the company's existence it is known some vehicles were given a uni-colour livery and the middle vehicle is in that livery or had perhaps already gained Southern green.

Pilton yard looks smart and pristine in this view. One of the three 2-6-2Ts built for the line in 1898 can just be seen poking out of the engine shed (*left*). The central shed marked No. 1 led to the carriage shop and roads 2 and 3 were a stone-walled carriage shed. The right-hand side tracks form the goods yard with the goods shed, doors shut, at the end. The water on the left is a mill leat.

Nash took a view of the far terminal at Lynton, a station that was always bedevilled by its location high above the sea and the settlement. The station was well founded. The engine shed is left, the layout was fully signalled and the goods shed and yard are in the distance. Everything is well tended and the platform is empty save for one soul. Just out of shot to the right was the signal box, its location betrayed by the point-rodding running under the track in the foreground. In 2003 the station building functioned as holiday accommodation, and the goods shed had become two cottages.

Exe and her crew were caught that Easter of 1924 at Lynton station. She appears highly burnished and retains the Lynton & Barnstaple Railway livery although by then owned by the Southern Railway. This was one of the three sister 2-6-2Ts turned out by Manning, Wardle in 1897/98 and which were held in great affection. Although the line closed over 65 years ago, it has exercised a strong hold over the railway lover's psyche. In recent years determined efforts have been made to recreate at least a part of the line with a replica 2-6-2T under construction, the station at Woody Bay renovated and even original rolling stock found rotting in fields and restored.

In 1926, the 17-year-old Nash must have enjoyed a memorable holiday to Jersey. He went there to stay with Aunt Mabel. Out came the camera to record two scenes on the 3 ft 6 in. gauge Jersey Railway. The photograph at St Aubins shows engine No. 2 (look at the chimney) *St Aubyns*. Along with sister No. 1, Manning, Wardle had built her in 1884. She was supplied at the time that the line was both converted from standard to 3 ft 6 in. gauge and extended from St Aubins to Corbière. This required the provision of a new and curving platform 3 at St Aubins for the extension. The original line ended in a train shed (removed in 1922) behind the fence to the left of the picture. A fire in this area in 1936 effectively closed the line by destroying 16 coaches. The chimney and dome of another engine in steam can just be made out in this area (look between the lady on the platform and No. 2's smokebox). To the right of the picture is the sea wall showing how restricted the layout was.

The second picture is extremely unusual. The location is the entry throat at St Aubins. The scene shows a Sentinel Cammell steam railcar in action and in the realms of the super-unusual it is hauling a trailer car. There were three Sentinel steam cars on the railway in 1926. It is thought that they had a yellow livery. Nash did not identify the car but owing to the position of the front duckets our suggestion is that this is No. 3 known either as *Wembley* or *La Moye*, which was delivered in 1925. The train is heading into the terminal platforms at St Aubins. One intriguing feature of the cars is that, like the railway's brake vans, they were fitted with letter boxes.

ASHOVER LIGHT RAILWAY.

TELEGRAMS:
ASHOVER RAILWAY, CLAYCROSS.

TELEPHONE No. 49 CLAY CROSS.

Secretary's and Manager's Office,
Clay Cross, Near Chesterfield,
July 8th 1926

Our Reference.	Your Reference.

Mr Nash has my permission
to walk the line and take any
photos he wishes on the Railway

John May

The Ravenglass escaped Grouping owing to its peculiar nature. The Jersey Railway off mainland Britain was not involved. Nor was a new narrow gauge railway, which did not open until 1925. During World War I an immense 2 ft gauge military railway system was created to service the Western Front. At the end of the war much of its equipment, some barely used, came into the Army Surplus category and was going for a song. One buyer was the Clay Cross Company through their subsidiary called The Ashover Light Railway. The company had bought the Overton estate in 1918, which was rich in minerals. To bring these to the works, the railway was created. Passenger traffic was an incidental diversion, although in the 1920s the line proved surprisingly popular at weekends. The passenger service, latterly summer only for a few days a week, ceased in 1936. The line closed in 1950. William Nash evidently determined in the summer of 1926 to see this unusual new phenomenon for himself: a completely new light railway on the narrow gauge with motor competition well established. He went to the trouble to get the manager's (John May) permission as this memo from July 1926 shows.

A feature of Ashover operation was the use of mixed trains. Here *Guy* heads an up 'mixed' at Woolley. Nowadays this area is under the water of Ogston Reservoir. The wagons are laden with the stone, which formed the core of the railway's traffic. *Guy* had a confusing persona. The line started out with four ex-War Department Baldwin 4-6-0Ts bought in 1922. The Clay Cross Company was family-owned and the locomotives carried the names of the owner's children. Even at the railway's opening two of the engines were reckoned as worn out. Another two were bought as replacements and nameplates were shunted around. The second *Guy* would have been quite fresh when Nash saw it. The engine itself was withdrawn in 1936 although its remains lingered for years.

The rural Ashover terminus featured a complete triangle, as did Clay Cross enabling entire trains to turn. In this picture *Peggy* is at the end of the Ashover triangle. In front of the engine is driver Reg Ling who it is known was only a railway worker between April 1925 and August 1926.

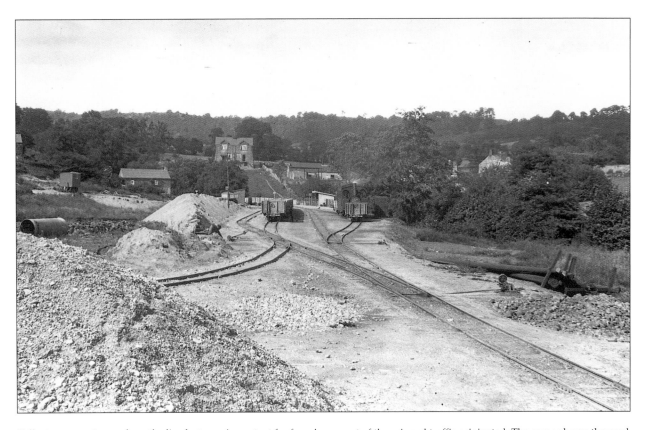

Fallgate was part way along the line but very important for from here most of the mineral traffic originated. The scene shows the yard looking towards Ashover. The station building is visible in the distance between the wagons. An engine lurks on the right-hand track. The spur to the left led to the mines, which went into the hillside on the left. After the line closed in 1950 elements of the layout survived at Fallgate with around 20 wagons to service the fluorspar plant. This was diesel-worked and lasted to about 1969.

This view at Fallgate is of *Joan*. The relatively fresh paintwork on the stock is noticeable. A little touch that has excited Ashover historians is the bell on the smokebox. It had gone in a published photo from October 1926 to leave just the fixing bolt visible. The brackets right at the front of the smokebox top carried an (evidently optional) lamp. *Joan* did not quite reach the end, falling out of use around 1948. The coaches seen in the pictures come from a group of four saloon bogie vehicles that the line bought new from Gloucester Railway Carriage & Wagon Works in 1924. With a couple of converted wagons these handled most of the traffic, supplemented after 1926 by some second-hand coaches from the Neverstop Railway at the Wembley Empire Exhibition.

A view of *Joan* and passenger train at Ashover. On the engine is Harold Skinner who it is known started on the line on Whit Monday 1926. That bell is prominent again.

The Ashover system was on the eastern edge of the Peak District. Further west, there was another public narrow gauge railway called the Leek & Manifold Valley Light Railway (L&M). As a subsidiary of the North Staffordshire Railway, this line, which opened in 1904, was, when Nash knew it, part of the LMS. The two pictures in his collection are both reproduced and date from 1926. Both are at the upper terminus of Hulme End. This is the subject of the first and general view. Behind the photographer, the three tracks running out of the shot rapidly became one and the setting was one of surrounding hills. The tracks in the station area were level but from the throat dropped away at 1 in 73. A double-armed signal guarded this approach and with the initial set of points was worked from the ground frame visible left. Sidings for handling goods are on the left under the loading gauge. This was set for something in excess of standard gauge despite the line's 2 ft 6 in. gauge. This was because each track ended in a length of standard gauge track and that was because of a very unusual L&M feature, the use of transporter trucks. That technology was the brainchild of the Manifold's engineer E.R. Calthrop. He was essentially an Indian railway engineer for whom the Manifold acted as a showcase. Even the sole bogie goods van No. 3, seen in front of a coal truck-carrying transporter, was Indian in style. The Manifold proved Calthrop's ideas about transporter trucks, which were then adopted by the Barsi Light Railway in India. In Nash's picture a loaded transporter is in the passenger platform in front of a carriage. Another one, as mentioned, is to its left and at least a couple of standard gauge goods trucks are on their own rails beyond that. Nash does not afford us a fine photograph of a carriage but the steel frames to the right of the tracks do join the passenger carrying theme. On popular summer days (Nash's looks wet) the four coaches were overburdened. These frames with attached canopies were used to convert the goods opens and transporters into temporary coaches. Between the stock in the station and these frames, more features are in the distance. Engine No. 1 *E.R. Calthrop* can just be made out and is the subject of the next picture. He sits in front of the engine shed and to the right of that is the carriage shed, for the line's operational base was here and not at the standard gauge connection at Waterhouses. Thus a large water tank and coaling stage are also features.

The second picture moves close into the shed where sits *E.R. Calthrop* in LMS livery. The line was run by two identical Kitson-built 2-6-4Ts. They were smaller versions of a Calthrop 4-8-4T design for the Barsi Light Railway. The massive nameplates were distinctive and all four plates survived the scrapping of the engines. The travelling hoist for maintaining the engines and the base of the water tower are prominent as is another loaded transporter wagon. After closure in 1934 much of the route became a public footpath in 1937 and remains such, although one length including the tunnel at Swainsley is a public highway.

Chapter Six

The Year of the General Strike: 1926

On three counts 1926 proved momentous for Nash. It started with his leaving school, it became the year of the General Strike in which he was a strikebreaking volunteer for the LMS, and by the year's end he had applied for a job with that railway.

In the inter-war period many individuals with a privileged upbringing reacted in their own ways to the growing realisation of the unacceptability of large scale poverty. George Orwell wrote *The Road to Wigan Pier*, W.H. Auden involved himself with the left. William Nash's reaction was perhaps less flamboyant but nevertheless worthy. He was an individual of religious conviction, one whose later attachment to Esperanto confirmed his internationalist credentials but he was also a product of the British private school system. Nash's conclusion to a year of turmoil would see him take a job on the bottom rung of the LMS ladder but in his home county of Cumberland. This period of upheaval had started for William in the autumn of 1925 when he caught measles followed by a kidney ailment – which would trouble him for the rest of his life. He was bed bound for 12 weeks; aware of his mother's pecuniary predicament in the New Year of 1926, he did not return to Radley College despite excellent school reports. During his recuperation he started to learn shorthand and typing as preparation for a railway career.

Right: Medal awarded by the LMS to William Nash for his work during the General Strike in the Alstone Junction signal box, Cheltenham.

Nash was able to get away from the turmoil at times in 1926, one good escape being a journey to Jersey. This took him through Weymouth where he composed this charmingly detailed view of Weymouth Quay full of holiday interest as a boat train connection to the Channel Islands arrives which Nash photographed from the steamer itself. Beyond the image, the content is layered with interest. The carriages have legible Channel Islands Boat Express boards. Then study the join between the second and third coaches. They are articulated together and were used here between 1925-34. The articulation obviated the use of special couplings, which the sharp curves of the tramway required and which had to be fitted every time coaches joined or left the tramway. The quayside tramway at Weymouth always fascinated and remains in existence today. Lightweight engines had to be used and the one in the picture was a newcomer on the job. Named *Kidwelly*, this was an Avonside of Bristol-built industrial engine, which the Great Western Railway gained from the Burry Port and Gwendraeth Valley Railway in 1922. The engine worked from 1903-1953 and first came to Weymouth in 1926, the year in which Nash took his picture. During the 1920s the arrangements at Weymouth Quay for handling both trains and ships proved very cramped and between 1931-33 the arrangements were completely rebuilt.

We cannot be sure how Nash came to Weymouth; since the engine is pulling in with a Great Western train, it is possible his route was down the South Western main line from the Basingstoke area. That is by way of introduction to pictures taken at other times in 1926 of Parkstone and Basingstoke. Parkstone between Bournemouth and Poole was located part way along the two mile Parkstone Bank of 1 in 60 broken only by 1 in 300 through the station. The change of grade can be seen along this eastbound Weymouth to Waterloo express. Within the length of the station the line changed from embankment to cutting. The engine is Southern Railway No. 560E. A member of the Adams 'T3' class 4-4-0 built for the London & South Western Railway in 1892, sister engine No. 563 survives as part of the National Railway Museum collection. The class had ended normal service in 1945 but in Nash's time were still entrusted with main line expresses despite their diminutive stature. Nash frames the train with plenty of detail from (*left*) the LSWR cast sign, the concrete components (the inter-war Southern widely used concrete), the loading gauge, the LSWR lattice post signals, the enamel signs and signal box (*right*). The loading gauge was placed at the exit of the goods yard, which is off to the left where there was also a connection to the private line of the South Western Pottery Company.

The majority of trains passing Parkstone were green but until 1930 distinctive blue trains run by the Somerset & Dorset Joint Railway (S&D) were a feature. The S&D service carried on until 1966 but in 1930 this joint LMS/SR railway handed over operations to its partners. Nash made sure an S&D train was photographed as their engine, No. 15, ran through with a Burnham-on-Sea to Bournemouth train. The engine in blue was, notwithstanding, a classic Derby production. A four strong batch including No. 15 had been designed by Johnson in 1891, although by Nash's time it had been substantially rebuilt by Deeley. The exposed springing on the tender frames lends an antique feel. The class was extinct by 1932. The vantage point for the image is much further up the same platform than the previous image.

Basingstoke platform end at the down end was an excellent vantage point. No. 778E *Sir Pelleas* hauls an Exeter to London Waterloo express in 1926. This 'King Arthur' class engine had started its 34 year life in 1925 and is seen before the fitting of smoke deflectors. This marvellous series of names started to appear in 1925 although the story is complicated in that some of the 'N15' class engines so named went back to 1918. Did the Southern's naming policy have any connection with the foundation of the Round Table movement in Norwich in 1927? The second such club was formed in Portsmouth. At the least, the climate of the 1920s turned the naming policy into an inspiration. W.H. Auden wrote in *A Cave of Making* in 1964 '. . . both of us, became self conscious at a moment when locomotives were named after knights in Mallory'. To the left is one of Basingstoke's famous electro-pneumatic signal gantries underneath which lies the goods yard and the West (or 'B') signal box in the distance. To the right of *Sir Pelleas* is the 1905-1967 engine shed and in front of that No. 594 with two horseboxes. This engine is an Adams 'X2' class 4-4-0 built for the LSWR in the early 1890s, examples of which were still active in World War II. The electro-pneumatic signals were a feature here from 1906 to 1966. The air cylinders are on the frames beneath each arm. They were an early form of power signalling supplied by the British Pneumatic Railway Signal Co.

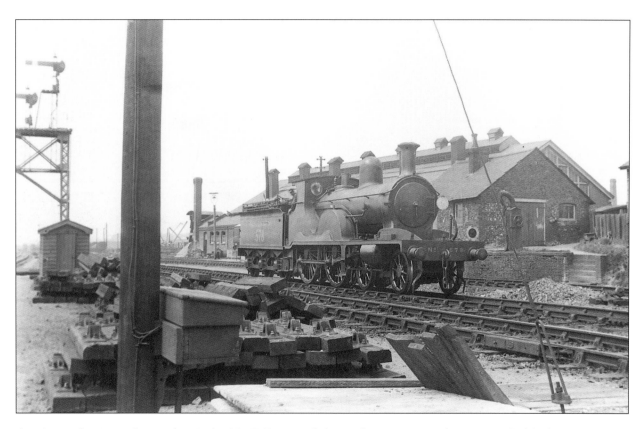

A variant on the view at the same location has No. 578E running light into the station. Again there is a wonderful collection of clutter. The engine was the second class member of William Adams' graceful 7 ft 1 in. driving wheel 'X2' class. The E suffix to the number indicated Eastleigh works and meant therefore a former London & South Western section engine, or in the case of the new builds like the 'King Arthurs', one allocated for work there. A unified locomotive number system was not adopted by the Southern until 1931.

Back with the theme of the main line looking west, there are three key differences from two photographs previously. No. 513E is one of the small driving-wheeled family of Urie 4-6-0, an 'S15' class designed really for goods. It was new in 1921 and is hauling a three-coach local set. Beside it is one of the Adams 'O2' class 0-4-4T whose relatively clean livery still proclaims 'LSWR' on the tank sides. Basingstoke's pneumatic signal gantries were to be seen on movie film as Will Hay's *Oh! Mr Porter* reached its climax in the station.

'King Arthur' class No. 791E *Sir Uwaine* on a Bournemouth-bound express. The location is the London end of Basingstoke station. The electro-pneumatic signalling did away with mechanical point rodding and signal wires even for the small shunting signals. Instead a pressurised piping network was needed. Two signal boxes are visible either side of the engine. That on the right is the East or 'A' box and just visible to the engine's right is the 'C' box, which controlled the junction with the Great Western's route to Reading. The GWR had its own station and goods yard in which GW-liveried wagons can be discerned. Behind *Sir Uwaine's* smokebox in the vee of the junction would appear the 1960s power signal box, which, with electrification of the line in 1966-67, would sweep the steam era away. Lost before that modernisation blitz (about 1950) was the GWR engine shed visible above the wagons.

Seen in the body of Basingstoke station, it is *Sir Pelleas* again hauling an express bound for the West of England. For the 'King Arthurs', the 1926 coal strike brought grief as supplies of Welsh steam coal dried up. Some had to be fitted up for oil firing. The same year also saw the start of fitting smoke deflectors, which changed the front end appearance considerably.

Nash's album numbers suggest that in July-August 1926 when it is known he made his visit to the Ashover Light Railway shown in the previous chapter, he was able to add in some time beside the Midland Railway main line through the Peak District at Darley Dale and Rowsley. This line would shut in 1968 although this section has been rebuilt by Peak Rail. Nash made much of the railway hardware in these compositions, both chosen images at Darley Dale focus on the Midland Railway cast trespass sign, one on the end of each platform looking north. These signs and the Midland Railway lower quadrant signals remained in place until closure. The background to the first image has former Midland Compound '4P' No. 1016, which had been built at Derby in 1906. Far away in the distance at the end of the loops can just be made out Church Lane Crossing with its signal box and footbridge.

The second Darley Dale image caught LMS No. 333. This was another version of the multifarious Midland Railway '2P' type, in this case coming from a class of 30 originally built in 1882-83 but having been rebuilt by Deeley from 1904. The group was known as the '1562' class (from the pre-1907 numbering) and this engine had received its rebuild in 1906, which had totally transformed its outline. Its 1906 form took it through to its condemnation, which took place, within months of Nash's picture, during 1926.

Four of Nash's five images of Rowsley are all versions of this composition. The engines were all Midland Railway design Compounds but two (including No. 1038 here) are specially related to the summer of 1926. The engine is burning oil, the tanks for which can just be seen in the tender. The incidental feature of water column (*left*) and semaphore signal (*right*) have an extra nuance in that the signal is representative of Midland practice that would fall out of favour in LMS days, whereby arms controlling each direction of traffic were mounted on one post.

This look at Nash's pictures in strike year 1926 concludes, unsurprisingly, with a selection from the Cheltenham area. First, comes a view from beside the signal box at Charlton Kings south-east of Cheltenham. GWR No. 1125 is running through and the significance of this is that it is one of the rare former Midland and South Western Junction Railway 4-4-0 engines. The engine existed between 1911 and 1932. Some of these former MSWJR engines were thoroughly Swindonised with taper boiler and Swindon cab. Not so No. 1125 (formerly No. 7) which went for overhaul at Swindon in October 1924 and was given a Swindon superheater with its MSWJR boiler, and a GWR chimney. It was left otherwise unscathed.

Next in Nash's album list and seemingly taken soon after the previous photograph is something of a show stopper on what looks like a warm summer's day. GWR 'Bird' series 'Bulldog' 4-4-0 No. 3449 *Nightingale* and 2-6-0 No. 5310 are storming through Charlton Kings with what Nash captioned as the Barry to Newcastle passenger train. He noted that it was composed of LNER stock. The train was making its way cross-country towards Banbury and the ex-Great Central route north. For decades (apart from wartime) this train was the daily event on the otherwise sleepy cross-country GWR route from Cheltenham to Banbury through Kingham and Chipping Norton. It called at Gloucester, avoided Cheltenham proper by calling at Cheltenham South & Leckhampton and used a flyover cut-off to avoid Kingham. Although this train ran again after World War II, it was routed via Swindon and Oxford.

It is thought that GWR No. 1004 has just crossed the 200 ft contour not far out of Cheltenham on the pull up into the Cotswolds with a Midland & South Western Junction route service to Andover. The path visible in the foreground is a useful locating factor used with old Ordnance Survey maps. This area is now built over. The engine had been MSWJR No. 20, an 0-6-0 from Beyer, Peacock in 1899. With its nine other class members, these were all heavily rebuilt and Swindonised in 1925-27 and it must have been fresh from this process when Nash photographed it.

Wonderfully evocative of the Great Western goods is this scene of one of Dean's outside-framed (spot the whirling cranks) goods engines passing Leckhampton near Cheltenham on its way to Kingham. Dean's single-framed goods engines were numerous and lasted until 1957 with one preserved. This version only existed in a 20-strong class built in 1885/86. Although the class was still intact in 1926, withdrawals started a couple of years later and all were gone by 1946.

Whilst many of Nash's Cheltenham pictures were taken either just south-west of Lansdown or along the Kingham branch, there is some representation for the Honeybourne line. This was a main line, which the GWR built, connecting Cheltenham and Honeybourne to give the GWR better connections between the West Midlands and the Lower Severn Valley. It was not opened until 1906 and never having been the busiest of routes was progressively closed by BR, only for much of it (including the part through this scene at Bishop's Cleeve) to be re-constructed as the Gloucestershire Warwickshire Railway with Cheltenham Racecourse station regaining its services and becoming a terminus in 2003. In addition to through services the GWR tried to foster local traffic. A railmotor service existed from the outset and even as late as 1928 the GWR opened a new halt at Hayles Abbey. At Bishop's Cleeve passenger traffic ceased in 1960 although BR trains of various sorts continued to pass until 1976. Nash photographed 0-6-0ST No. 1040 hauling two autocars on the local service, which ran between Honeybourne and Cheltenham.

Nash noted this as a Paddington to Cheltenham working approaching Cheltenham. It is a charming picture but the researcher's eye is caught by the engine number Nash noted. GWR No. 3555 must have been one of the most rebuilt engines in history. It was one of 40 Dean '3521' class 4-4-0s. It had started life as a 7 ft 0¼ in. gauge 0-4-2ST in 1889. After a couple of years it became an 0-4-4T before being converted to standard gauge when the broad gauge was abandoned in 1892. After less than a decade in that state, the engine was turned right around and converted into a 4-4-0 tender engine. This particular engine spent 29 years as a 4-4-0 before condemnation in 1929, three years after this picture was taken.

Despite the recovery in 2002 of Nash's photographic notebook, a number of his images continue to pose questions. A group known as Album 177-188 are a case in point. No negatives have been traced and where they are reproduced, it has been by scanning the contact print. Their dating is also a challenge although they are likely to be either from 1926 or possibly 1927. Two of these close this chapter. The first shows a Bradford to Paignton train near Cheltenham. Whether north or south of the town we cannot say, although possibly the Midland Railway cast-iron notice might suggest the north? The interest in the image is partly the double-header storming along behind two '2P' 4-4-0s LMS Nos. 520 and 522. This is enhanced because the tanks in the tender confirm that the lead engine No. 522 is burning oil (as the smoke might also suggest!). A few images previously, another ex-Midland oil burner was seen at Rowsley.

Evidently heavy passenger trains appealed to Nash in the Cheltenham area; freights were photographed but not as frequently. An exception is this 'over the boundary fence' view of the Cheltenham Lansdown sidings. Passing with a laden coal train is an ex-Midland 0-6-0 LMS No. 2465. This was one of Kirtley's '1F' freight engines. The large class of 470 were built over 11 years from 1863 and the last continued in use until 1951. Even in the 1920s, their outside frames curved over the coupling rod cranks and outside-framed tenders looked very antiquated. Two passenger trains of GWR stock are in the sidings behind. The locomotive visible above No. 2465's tender is GWR No. 1126, another representation for the former M&SWJR 4-4-0s. Nash noted that this train was to form the 10.28 am to Southampton. Rather obscured by its own steam under the middle signal post is an ex-Midland 0-4-4T No. 1361. Is the presence of these GWR trains on what was firm Midland territory surprising? Not when it is remembered that the M&SWJR was in many ways a friend of the Midland Railway and for connectional purposes used the Midland's Lansdown station. The M&SWJR services continued to use Lansdown until track alterations in 1958 meant that the final few years of the service ran from the former GWR Cheltenham St James' terminal station. It seems that to take this image Nash must have been standing on the rails of the branch tramway that accessed the Cheltenham & District Tramways St Mark's depot and which closed in 1930.

Chapter Seven

To Work on the Railway: 1927

W. K. Nash.

Date of birth   January 11, 1909.
Date entered service February 24, 1927.

Station	Period	Work performed
Arnside	10 months during 1927-8-9.	General station work including: Booking passengers; collection acceptance, carriage, and delivery of parcels, goods, and minerals. Telegraph. All station accounts including: Stamps, waybills, invoices, abstracts, posting all relative books, ledgers, public accounts, train registers, daily balances, weekly and monthly returns up to and including the Accounts Current, Passenger (twice) and Goods (once). Also lost property, gas, water, etc. returns. Station and yard working, including loading and labelling of wagons.
Newby Bridge	6 weeks 1927.	Summer clerk (under supervision of Lakeside).
Greenodd	4 weeks 1927.	General station working and accounts.
Windermere	3 months 1927.	Stationmaster's Office work including: Public correspondence and inquiries. Seat and compartment reservations.
Carnforth	1½ years during 1927-30.	Booking and parcels office. Stationmaster's office, including: Custody of correspondence, writing up time-signature books, time-sheets, preparation of salary-lists, wages paybills, and all returns relative thereto. Staff rosters. District Control Office, including: Recording and regulation of traffic. Relief of trainmen. Distribution of rolling-stock. Goods Guards' Clerk's work. Summer relief from Carnforth.
Crewe	2½ years during 1928 and 1929-30.	General work in Trains Office and Divisional Passenger Control Office.
Swansea	May 29, 1933.	District Runner.
Crewe	April 23. 1934.	Head Office Inspector. (Passenger Trains).
	Feb. 18. 1935.	Assistant Distributor of Rolling Stock.
Euston	May 11. 1936.	Time-table Clerk, Commercial Dept.
	September 29. 1936.	Electrification ", - .

2

Particulars of relief experience.

Relief at	Work performed
Morecambe (Prom)	Parcels.
Lancaster (C.& G.A.)	Passenger and parcels.
Arkholme	) Vice Stationmaster sick. Temporarily under
Borwick	) supervision of Carnforth.
Settle.	General station.
Leeds (Wellington)	Parcels.
Silverdale (Lancs)	General station.
Grange over Sands	Passenger and parcels.
Sandside	General station.
Oxenholme	
Kendal	Parcels.
Tebay	Stationmaster's office.
Threlkeld	General station, including preparation of Goods Account Current, April, 1930.
Keswick	Passenger and parcels.

General:

I have prepared timetables, train and carriage diagrams. Am acquainted with engine and guards' diagrams, etc

I have been a member of the Company's Signalling classes for three years, and hold three signalling certificates, first class with distinction, namely, preliminary, advanced, and Honours.

I have also about sixty hours practical experience in a signalbox.

On 24th February, 1927 Nash's life as a salaried employee of the LMS started as a clerk. As a junior clerk he was allocated to various Cumbrian stations. Between 1927 and 1930, he spent time at Arnside, Newby Bridge, Carnforth, Greenodd and Windermere stations. Since the publication of *Cumbrian Railway Photographer*, Nash's notebook dating his images has been recovered. The notebook reveals that no railway pictures were taken in 1927. It seems as if his junior position on the railway suggested to him he should put his camera away. It was not until February 1928 that he started taking pictures again with a series taken around Carnforth. Addresses from December 1928 to 1930 suggest he was working for periods again at Carnforth. Meanwhile during May/June 1928 he had managed a photo stint in the Crewe area.

Much of Nash's photographic work from the Carnforth-Arnside area is reproduced in *Cumbrian Railway Photographer*. One that was not, partly because no original negative survives, is this view of former Furness Baltic tank No. 117, now LMS No. 11102, at Carnforth Furness & Midland Junction with the 10.45 am Carnforth to Grange passenger train. The image was taken in February 1928.

Anyone aspiring to a management position with the LMS would have wanted to spend time at Crewe. Some correspondence indicates that from 1st March, 1928 he was formally within the office of the divisional operating superintendent at Crewe although he continued to work at various locations. He qualified as a signalman as part of the process. This position probably explains how he got access for a whole series of pictures taken from inside the railway fence on the four track section of main line south of Crewe around Basford Hall and Betley Road. Nash dates this sequence for May 1928. The first selection is a straightforward view of something which would become common but which must have given anyone of LNWR sensibilities (not that Nash ever seemed biased) cause for thought. An archetypal Midland Railway design '4F' 0-6-0 is wheeling a down express goods along the LNWR main line. The engine is No. 4437 which was new in 1927, just months old when Nash encountered it in early May 1928.

Another location used by Nash was Betley Road, further south than Basford Hall. Once again he's inside the boundary fence and perhaps there as a result of a tip off because his annotation revealed that LMS (so liveried) Nos. 5064 and 6761 were out on a trial trip. Presumably it was the 2-4-0 No. 5064 on a trial? This had been LNWR 'Precedent' class No. 1187 *Chandros*. Yeadon's *Compendium* records that it gained its LMS number in March 1927, three and a half years before withdrawal. How does this relate to this 5th May, 1928 image in denoting a spring visit to Crewe works? The livery, although LMS, remained black but an LMS style smokebox number plate is fitted.

Betley Road is the location for this view of the 2.45 pm Liverpool to Birmingham train on the 5th May, 1928. The engine in LMS livery is No. 5339 *Henry Maudslay*. This was a LNWR 'George the Fifth' class 4-4-0. These were reasonably successful engines and 90 were built despite which many did not have overlong lives. This engine only existed between 1911 and 1937 having gained its LMS livery in December 1927, so once again some interest is in the livery transition. Henry Maudslay was a Victorian mechanical engineer closely associated with Brunel of whom L.T.C. Rolt remarked 'No man exercised a greater influence on mechanical engineering practice throughout the 19th century than Henry Maudslay'. The 'George the Fifths' became very familiar to children owing to the exceptional number of contemporary model railway manufacturers who made models of the class, the patriotic series of names perhaps appealing. There is also interest in the marvellous 12-wheeled coach at the head of the train. It is one of the little-photographed Caledonian Railway 'Grampian' corridor coaches of 1905 which 20-plus years on had strayed a long way from home territory.

Nash had an eye for the unusual and an attraction in the Crewe area were the former North Staffordshire Railway (NSR) engines, several of which he was to photograph over time. This image from 2nd June, 1928 was noted as the 1.10 pm Weston & Ingestre to Crewe near Crewe behind LMS No. 2252. There is some negative damage to what otherwise seems to have been a successful photograph. Weston & Ingestre was a station on the former North Staffordshire south of Stone, so what Nash saw was a local service which had made its passage through the Potteries. Weston was to lose its passenger trains as long ago as January 1947. No. 2252, the erstwhile North Staffordshire No. 95, was one of their relatively abundant class 'L' 0-6-2Ts. The class had totalled 34 but the LMS had got rid of them all by 1937. This engine had a short life between 1909 and 1934 and unlike some sisters, including one still in existence, was not sold for further use in industry.

Another local train caught by Nash near Crewe on 2nd June, 1928 was a further North Staffordshire service, this time the 3 pm from Crewe to Blythe Bridge, south-east of the Potteries and still open. A much less common example of former North Staffordshire locomotive power is at the head. The engine is 2-4-2T No. 1458 once NSR No. 24. This was a much longer-lived engine than the preceding example. Life had started in 1886 as a Clare 2-4-0T which Longbottom had rebuilt as a 2-4-2T in 1901, in which state it worked until 1934.

Hauling a third North Staffordshire service from the 2nd June, 1928, there is an example of a design that Nash would photograph again (see later in this chapter). With good reason, for the North Staffordshire 0-6-4Ts were distinctive engines. There were actually two classes with this unusual wheel arrangement. Both were built in World War I and this engine LMS No. 2064, the old No. 4, came out in 1915. Technically these class 'C' were classified as freight engines unlike their class 'F' siblings. As the photograph shows it did not make much difference despite their smaller driving wheels. The engine lasted until 1937. The train was the 2.55 pm Stoke to Crewe.

Nash photographed the 12.20 pm from Holyhead to London Euston as it approached Crewe station behind an un-named 'Claughton', LMS No. 5972 - an engine that only worked for 17 years between 1920-37. The picture was taken on the 10th June, 1928 and that April the engine had been re-boilered with a larger boiler as is visible. What makes the photograph so impressive is the accompanying railwayana. A lamp and shunting engine to the right, signal gantry and chimney to the left and, dominating the picture along with the engine, a suspension bridge disappearing into the building behind the engine. This was no ordinary affair, it was called The Spider Bridge and it bisected Crewe North signal box behind No. 5972. Constructed in 1878, it carried a narrow gauge railway and footpath connecting the station and the works. This was an impressive part of the Crewe scenery although the narrow gauge railway had been disused for several years before the bridge's demolition in 1939.

A straightforward side-on shot of LMS No. 13037 at Crewe on the 23rd June, 1928. The engine would have been about 18 months old when Nash photographed it and already looks well worn with both number and LMS insignia apparently obscured. One of the Horwich 'Crabs', it would remain in traffic until November 1966, an example of the first significant LMS design that owed little to pre-Grouping practice with a total of 245 engines built.

Nash evidently made another trip south from Cumbria in September 1928 when his notebook records photos taken at Derby and Stoke-on-Trent on 6th September. The two at Stoke hold their interest in representing former North Staffordshire Railway engines. Nash noted LMS No. 2050 as being on an up passenger train with no other detail. It is a member of passenger class 'F' 0-6-4T (unlike the smaller-wheeled class 'C' from three photos back). It had a service life of less than 20 years between 1916-1935.

Stoke is the venue for this example of an ex-North Staffordshire 0-4-4T LMS No. 1435. That wheel arrangement was popular with several companies for passenger tank engines and the NSR had nine. This one from class 'M' worked from 1908-1930. I wonder whether the livery is crimson lake? It is certainly lined (see the tank sides) and there is an LMS emblem on the bunker. The livery style is therefore older than the 0-6-4T in the preceding picture and as a passenger engine it is possible that an early repaint by the LMS had been in the crimson lake. It is known that North Staffordshire passenger engines including tanks received this livery. Two members of the 'M' class became the last NSR steam engines in use by the LMS in 1939.

These visits to the hub of the LMS at Crewe (at least in some eyes) had commenced the year after his employment had started. Nash certainly lived in Arnside in the late 1920s, working, so it seems, frequently at Carnforth station. In his photographic notebook Nash records no pictures at all for 1929. A small group at Arnside (with examples in *Cumbrian Railway Photographer*) were taken on the 26th November, 1928. Thereafter nothing was taken in 1929 and indeed nothing until June 1931 apart from a sequence of eight in January 1930 at Carnforth (again, with examples in *Cumbrian Railway Photographer*). One from that Carnforth group that was not used is reproduced here to close the chapter in which Nash commenced his salaried life with the LMS. The photograph shows former Furness Railway 0-6-0 No. 2, now LMS No. 12495, in the sidings at Carnforth Furness and Midland Railway Junction with a goods train from Grange-over-Sands on the frosty 28th January, 1930. This was a relatively sizeable and modern Pettigrew '3F' freight engine some of which (not 12495) would last into BR days.

Chapter Eight

Management Trainee

In June 1930 Nash's formal address moved to Crewe (109 Catherine Street) and by now it was clear he was embarking on a management career with the LMS. Initially he was in lodgings but in March 1932 he rented a house for himself and his mother at 50 Claughton Avenue, named in honour of the LNWR's Chairman during the decade from 1911. Certain of these dates differ from those quoted in *Cumbrian Railway Photographer*. That August of 1932 he was out with his camera around the station. One of his images caught LMS-built '4P' Compound No. 1170 of 1925 hauling the 3.05 pm Manchester to Birmingham out of the station.

Another 4-4-0 to come in front of the camera that month was an altogether rarer example of the genre. LMS No. 5413 seen shunting around the station was once North Staffordshire Railway No. 171, a 1910 engine from a five strong class. Her withdrawal would take place the next year and the number 5413 had only been applied in 1928 when her first LMS number 598 was required for one of the new build of MR design '2P' 4-4-0.

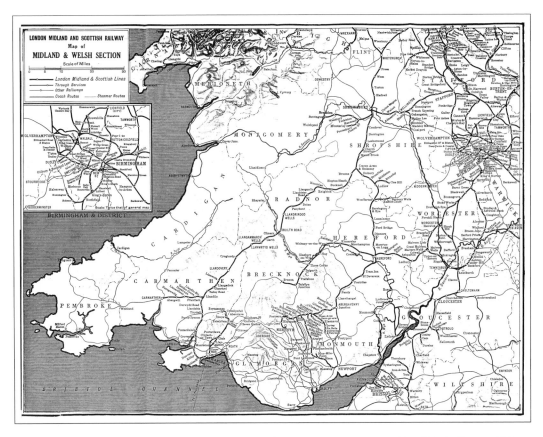

After nearly three years at Crewe, Nash moved again, this time to the Swansea area in June 1933 as District Runner. This was a sort of ancestor to a modern day Management Training Scheme. His move led – as appears to have happened before – to a hiatus in train photography. Only two railway photos were taken in 1933 (see next chapter). Other memorabilia survives from the South Wales period. One is this fine LMS map focusing on their South Wales system, which would have come from a timetable.

Nash had various foibles and this letter illustrates two (at least). Wherever he lived, he sought to perpetuate the memory of his clerical grandfather, the rector of Somerby by Grantham. Even though he only rented a house in Swansea, he renamed it. He had around 1926/27 taught himself to type and made carbons of his correspondence. Ever resourceful and economical, he grabbed handfuls of out of date LMS handbills and used their reverses for his carbons. Today it is hard to know which has more value: the handbill, perhaps for some noteworthy football match and special trains thereto, or the correspondence.

This particular letter written towards the end of his time in Swansea was addressed to one of his mentors, Mr Sykes, the station master at Windermere. It reveals he had two core responsibilities: organising coaching stock and dealing with publicity including poster displays. How many people combine those jobs on the 21st century railway?

Somerby
Goitre Fawr Road
Dunvant
Swansea
February 10, 1934

Dear Mr Sykes

It really is past time that I should write to you, but I have hardly known whether I stood on my head or my heels since I've been down here. We'll take the job first.

I worked a great deal of overtime up to the end of October in the process of getting the job straight. I deal with anything that is handed out to me, and have two particular functions, coaching stock in sets and all workings, i.e. marshalling circular and carriage diagram, and outdoor publicity.

I found on arrival in my current correspondence basket, pads of letters about coaches in which the date of the last letter was as far back as January 1932! They were in any order; I perused them, and reduced them from about 3″ thick to about 8 sheets of paper. I now have a pad for each set, filed in alphabetical and number order. The record of stock in sets was a narrow cash-book, so much crossed out, daggered in, circled and squared, that I couldn't read it, so I have card-index in my pocket, so that whenever I see a set I can check it up. The system is simplicity and reliability itself. In the sphere of publicity I had passed on to me only four records, three of which were inaccurate, and the other inaccurate and messy. I have redrafted these and added eleven others, binding the whole in a black spring-back binder, which has made a job which earned the approval of Mr Roberts, the District Manager, and interested him for half-an-hour. He has been very kind and got me a pass for my bicycle, which enables me to do more work in more comfort, and at the same time to get exercise. He told me that my place was outside for the maximum possible time and, as far as my own work is concerned, gave me an absolutely free hand.

I have divided the District into nine circuits which I manage to get round in about a couple of months. When I visit a station I take with me a sheet showing all its poster-boards (a constant check on the census in my 'black book'), record all the posters exhibited and on hand spare, and obtain the answers to any questions I may have recorded at the foot of the sheet under the heading 'Special Items'.

These sheets are clipped together after the completion of each circuit, and constitute a record of all that I have seen and done. At the time of visiting a station I generally discuss the poster supply with the Stationmaster, and I have a blank sheet interleaved between each diary sheet for taking down his requirements. I always carry with me a list of what is in stock (an innovation) to enable them to assist in the selection of suitable posters for their stations.

I record every poster I distribute, ultimately, on a large sheet whose period coincides with a diary circuit period. The examination of these large sheets enables me to forecast my probable requirements for the various seasons with considerable accuracy. In this, however, I get no help from the Birmingham office, which acts as middleman between the printers and me. I applied at the end of August for sundry issues of pictorial posters, 'suitable for winter exhibition', and among the issues supplied were six bathing scenes! I wondered whether arrangements had been made for steam-heating the sea!

My periodical report for September and October created quite a stir (or shall I say? - a disturbance). I called attention to an aspect, a shocking aspect, of previous practice in poster distribution, which allowed stations to accumulate upwards (in two cases - Llandrindod Wells and Swansea St Thomas) of two hundred pictorial posters, many of them expensive R.A. Issues. To the exhibition of fares at all stations to one or more of four stations whose passenger train services had been withdrawn for years (Glanrhyd, Grovesend, Penclawdd, and Llanmorlais). To the absence of a fares list at Mumbles Road, in contravention of sect. 15 of the Regulation of Railways Act, 1868. To the fact that the point-to-point time for a fitted freight train between Llangunllo and Knighton is 13 minutes, and average speed of 30 mph, whereas the speed should be limited to 20 mph between Llangunllo Tunnel and Knighton by Appendix Instruction. To the complete non-observance of an Appendix Instruction about down passenger trains stopping at a certain part of the platform at Hopton Heath, owing to the narrowness of the platform beneath the overbridge three-quarters of the way along the platform. And to the working and signalling of the Fish train, 4.40 pm Swansea and 4.46 pm Carmarthen to Crewe, combined at Llandilo. The latter is a very interesting case, but requires some preliminary explanation. Nos. 3 and 4 headlights of our code, and their definitions are as follows.

No. 3   Parcels, newspaper, fish, meat, fruit, milk, horse, or perishable, train composed of coaching stock.
No. 4   Fitted freight, fish, or cattle, train with the continuous brake in use on not less than one-third of the vehicles.

To save specially requisitioning suitable coaching stock, the Swansea portion of this train is mainly formed of vacuum-fitted goods vans. As these cannot be regarded as coaching stock, the train could not carry No. 3 headlights, but the lights had to be reduced to No. 4 - 'Fitted Freight'. In addition, the traffic is passenger-rated.

As a freight train, the following conditions applied:

a)   The rear vehicle had to be a brake-van (Rule 153) (new Rule-book!!!)
b)   When assisted by an engine in the rear, the guard should remove the tail-lamp. In this case an additional stop should be made at Sugar Loaf Summit to enable the guard to replace the tail-lamp. (Rule 133) (The train is worked with a coaching brake-van.)

c)   The speed between Llangunllo Tunnel and Knighton should be restricted in accordance with Appendix Instruction to 20 mph, whereas the train is timed at 32½.

With regard to (a) Crewe Divisional Control have given instruction that Crewe fish must be marshalled behind the brake. (b) was not observed. (c) was habitually contravened.

The upshot is that Mr Ford has ruled that for the purpose of this definition, brake-fitted or piped goods and cattle wagons with not less than 9-ft wheelbase, may be regarded as coaching stock, so we now carry the 'parcels' lights, and all wrongs set out above are automatically set right.

Very regretfully I decided that I must give up all outside activities for a year after my removal here. It has meant a great loss to me, as we have thereby been deprived of opportunities of meeting many people, but I think the decision was wise: I really didn't know what demands the job would make on me. I had some signalling meetings with the Chief Staff Clerk (Atkinson, from Liverpool) before Christmas, at each other's house alternate weeks, but he is leaving shortly and we have not resumed them. Mr Roberts has asked me to lecture to schools on subjects of railway interest, so I was very busy for three weeks about Christmas and the New Year, preparing a paper to last about an hour. My first subject is 'Safety on the Railway', and the first paper will embrace outdoor signalling and interlocking. I went up to Mr Ashton Davies's office about it, and received instructions to stress the selling value of safety as much as possible. My Spanish is distinctly in the eclipse just now.

I've just had a month on an analysis of the position with regard to the loss of milk traffic in the Vale of Towy. Briefly the circumstances are as follows.

In November 1931 the River Towy bridges at Nantgaredig and Dryslwyn were washed away, cutting several farms off from their stations, except by long detours. A lorry operator stepped in, secured the traffic to Swansea (average 25 miles), extended his activities, and has now got away with five-sevenths of our dispatch. To get traffic back we must offer a gate-to-door service, if not yard-to-door. There are two possibilities, L.M.S. collection and delivery by road, with an intervening rail link, or L.M.S. lorries throughout. The former alternative is virtually ruled out because the accommodation at Llandilo, the geographical focus, for the transfer of the traffic between road and rail, is very poor, besides which it is a G.W. station. The second alternative, too, would enable the automobile units to be kept in more continuous work and in effect, the same units will be available for collection and delivery whereas, if a rail link intervenes, two fleets of lorries will be required.

I interviewed and categorised thirty-six farmers (What is your name? Who gave you this name? etc.) and found that the annual dispatch amounts to 654,358 gallons. At a proposed slightly reduced scale, the L.M.S. receipts would be increased by £1,828 if we could get back the whole of the traffic, but to do so would involve the provision of five lorries and seven sets of men, at a cost of £3,380, to perform the service, so I can't see it coming off. Anyway, I've to represent Mr Roberts at a meeting at the Adelphi at Liverpool on Wednesday, to 'ventilate' the whole matter. Mr Byrom seems to favour getting outside hauliers to act as our agents, preferably those who are competing with us now. I simply cannot understand what recommends our competitors as future allies, and have instructions to oppose the suggestion. My opinion is that it would be very unwise to entrust the name and reputation of the L.M.S. to an outside haulier, particularly one who has been antagonistic to us. I allow that each case must be treated on its own merits, but what do you think about it in principle?

Last week-end I was sent to Edinburgh in charge of a third-class sleeping and dining-car excursion, the 9.45 from Swansea on Friday evening! I heartily loathed the whole business, but it was a great success, the number of passengers conveyed by the eight trains being 2,055, including about 72 first-class in the 'posh' train, which was made up first-brake, two first sleeping-cars, first restaurant kitchen car, first vestibule, three first sleeping-cars, semiroyal saloon, and first brake lounge! I may say that this was filled practically by Mr Roberts's personal invitation. The whole effort made a substantial increase on the previous record.

I had two assistants to help me label my train on Friday morning, after which I came home and had an hour-and-a-half's rest on my bed, got up, fed, and caught the 7.15 pm down to the sidings. I had a last look-round, checked up the equipment, and we were drawn out on to the down main line for the 'posh' train to leave at 8.50, being berthed immediately afterwards at the platform which it had occupied. I may say that 180 local notabilities, including my Mama, received invitation to a state inspection of the 'posh' train before it left.

We were nine minutes early leaving Shrewsbury, ran into fog and the reaction of a breakloose at Winsford, with the result that we were 1 hr 25 mts late into Princes Street. I reported at the Stationmaster's Office and said I should not attend the banquet at the Caledonian Hotel, as I was feeling unwell. I caught my stock out to the stabling point, Seafield Branch in South Leith, which had been closed to traffic for the day. I turned into a berth and had seven hours rest. On getting up about 6 pm, the dining-car staff made me some tea, I relabelled my train, checked the equipment of all the berths (112 in number, four cars), locked the whole train, inside and out, turned out the lights, and went up past several other stabled trains to the first off, the 8.35 for 9.23 pm from Princes St. I made acquaintance of a platform on the way, but did no serious damage. The rear vehicle of the 8.35 stock was a Great Western saloon with bottom step board, into which I climbed just as it was moving off. I don't know what the C&W men thought!

I saw Mr Noel Phillips at Edinburgh; he seems to be enjoying his time in Scotland. On arrival at Princes Street once more, I left my bag at the Stationmaster's Office, together with a requisition for additional equipment, towels and soap, had another cup of tea and some sandwiches, and proceeded to the ticket barriers at 10 pm for duty. I chose No. 1, from which our 'posh' train was to return at 11.15. The preceding train was the 10.25 Great Western to the Western Valleys, and the cases of beer were brought up by barrow-loads. The crowd was unusually well-behaved; I saw only two men on the ground, and one fight, between two girls; a few merry souls conducted sundry choirs with bottles, but that was as far as it got. A policeman tried to expel me although I was on duty! A witness of the proceedings subsequently beckoned to me and discussed them; I told him I was merely carrying out orders; imagine my surprise when later I saw him go with his luggage to the 'posh' train.

My train, due to leave at 12.30 am was platformed about 12.15; my attendents looked after the passengers, while I remained at the barrier, No. 5 platform. About 12.24 I went to fetch my bag from the SMO and for the spare equipment from the linen room. I thrust the latter into the rear brakevan and was immediately set upon by an irate party who had, in spite of warning, left thirty-six bottles of beer in the compartment on arrival at Edinburgh, apparently thinking they would still be there on the return. I understand Sir Josiah Stamp is going to hear about it!

Mr Roberts takes over the duties of Docks Superintendent, Garston, on March 5th, so this little stunt will have been in the nature of his parting kick, to mix metaphors a bit. I understand he got a wonderful toast at the banquet, to the exclusion of Mr Ashton Davies who was also present. The Chairman of the Swansea Chamber of Commerce toasted the L.M.S. and Mr Roberts, 'the two being synonymous'. Mr Roberts has put Swansea on the map, and in large letters too; it is no longer, on the commercial side, a district for which any old thing is good enough. What he doesn't know about cultivating his customers isn't worth knowing. As far as organisation is concerned, the Great Western simply doesn't exist down here. The Swansea Staff will lose a good friend.

I had a very pleasant tour at the end of last May, from Macclesfield to Norwich, 280 miles, via Buxton, Chesterfield, Worksop, Lincoln, Horncastle, Boston, Kings Lynn, Hunstanton, Wells, Cromer, Aylsham, and East Dereham; it took me six-and-a-half-days. This June I'm promising myself a trip from Stranraer or Girvan, via Newton Stewart, Moniaive, Dumfries, Moffat, Selkirk, Hawick, and Langholm, to Carlisle. It will be a little shorter than last year, but the country will be more difficult.

Our new boss is Mr Tait from Abergavenny, who was the last L&NW superintendent here. The Abergavenny district office is to be closed, consequent upon the closer working with the Great Western, and the two districts will be administered from here. The closer working with the Great Western is an awful mess as far as Swansea Goods is concerned, because they really haven't adequate accommodation for their own shed traffic, let alone ours as well. I understand headquarters over-ruled the local superintendents, and the results bear witness of this.

I don't think I have any more news, except that I wish there wasn't such a long distance between Swansea and Windermere. I hope you are all keeping well.

Yours very sincerely

William Nash

Nash's letter was typed on the reverse of these handbills (*right*) for his carbon copy.

It was Easter Weekend of March 1934 before more photographs were listed. The train is the 4.07 pm from Hereford to Brecon behind LMS 0-6-2T No. 6936. The LNWR had had two substantial classes of 0-6-2T. The Webb 'Coal Tanks' were well known; one is still in existence from the 300 built. The other class had comprised 80 engines intended for passenger work known as the 'Watford Tanks'. It is former LNWR No. 2382 from this class that is seen here. Kinnersley station lay on an entirely isolated length of former Midland Railway between Hereford and Three Cocks Junction (south-west of Hay-on-Wye). It had been completed as the Hereford, Hay & Brecon in 1864 and fell into the Midland's hands in 1874. The reason for this was that just as the Central Wales line gave the LNWR a route to Swansea, this link gave the Midland, in conjunction with a couple of other companies, a route to the same destination. All of which was very relevant to Nash's career because of the time he was spending in the Swansea area on the LMS system inherited from these two former rivals. The line through Kinnersley closed in the 1960s.

Precisely following the Kinnersley image in Nash's records are two images from Hereford both of which are reproduced. The times given for the trains in this group of three would suggest that Nash stayed overnight in Hereford having come from the Swansea/Brecon direction. He was not more specific about the exact date in March 1934 but these two images are thought to be from Easter Monday. The first of the Hereford images shows the 8 am from Birmingham to Cardiff behind GWR 'Hall' class No. 4988 *Bulwell Hall*. This was a modern engine at the time. To its right is LMS No. 8908. This was a considerably older engine from the large build of LNWR 0-8-0 goods engines.

Many might think of Hereford as Great Western territory but as these three images suggest it was far more complicated. The Midland Railway was present as has been explained. The LNWR had arrived from the Shrewsbury direction through the jointly owned (with the Great Western) Shrewsbury and Hereford as part of its efforts to get into the South Wales coalfield. This explains the presence of the LNWR origin engine in the last photo and is confirmed by the sign on the goods depot in this photograph, a sign that had been updated to reflect the 1923 Grouping. One of the modern GWR 'Castle' class, No. 5019 *Treago Castle*, is passing through with the 9.15 am Liverpool-Plymouth.

Perhaps with his work in mind, Nash took a collection of images in South Wales concentrating on the stations and railway infrastructure. The infrastructure images started to appear from April 1934, ten months after he had arrived in South Wales and his last month there. The first in this sequence shows Gurnos. This was on the Swansea Vale Railway, a short but very complicated length of track, which the Midland Railway gained in 1874. Gurnos was towards the northern end, which terminated at Bryn Amman. It was not a passenger station but offered three other functions. It was a goods depot (*right*), a junction and one of the two Midland locomotive depots for this isolated network. The junction is in view, the tracks curving to the left to gain the Afon Twrch valley headed to Bryn Amman, whilst between the goods shed and the engine shed (*centre*), tracks can be seen heading under a bridge. This was a freight branch to Varteg. Note the double slip point in the foreground. Gurnos lost its railway with a sequence of closures in the mid-1960s.

This is Upper Bank in April 1934, the second depot for the Swansea Vale system. The shed had a typical allocation of Midland Railway '1F' 0-6-0Ts and later LMS Jinty '3F' 0-6-0Ts, examples of which are evident in both these pictures. One of the latter is hauling the freight train and there is evidence of locomotives at the shed from the steam in the centre of the photograph. Upper Bank's signal box is pure Midland; this was the first station out from the Midland's Swansea St Thomas terminus. Upper Bank was an important junction; the primary route is to the left (note the higher of the two junction signals is the left-hand at the platform end) and a passenger train from the Bryn Amman direction is approaching on the single line. A trainload of scrap waits. The tracks ahead of it were goods lines, which formed a loop for a few miles on the east side of the Tawe Valley. A large shed above the signal box carries the inscription 'Road & Rail Warehouse'. Despite the industrial nature of the area, the station seems clean and unvandalised, the waiting shelter to the left looking quite new. The forests of chimneys would be mainly associated with Swansea's tinplate industry. The system through Upper Bank started out as Scott's Tramroad in 1816, evolved considerably from around 1850, and whilst the passenger trains went in 1950 some freight continued through Upper Bank into the 1980s. The line was finally severed on the 21st May, 1983. Despite which, Upper Bank shed area retains railway interest having become the base for the Swansea Vale Railway Preservation Society. A mile and a half of track is involved north to Six Pit Junction.

Nash took two pictures of the Midland at Swansea St Thomas in April 1934 and they reveal how greatly motivated by coal traffic the presence of the Midland at Swansea was. The terminus is in the distance and the signal box can just be seen. The image looks south out to sea with the tidal River Tawe out of sight but present just behind the right-hand signal in the lower (clear) position. This was controlling a short branch, which crossed the Tawe to access docks and industrial premises.

Across the Tawe on the west bank near the South Dock was the rival LNWR Swansea Victoria terminus. One day in April 1934 Nash captured two Fowler 2-6-4Ts working together, they were then only a few months old. Engines Nos. 2390 and 2403 are departing Swansea Victoria with the 10.15 am over the Central Wales route to Stafford. No. 2390 went into traffic in June 1933, No. 2403 in September 1933. The prominent lower quadrant semaphore signals were classic London & North Western Railway equipment. A different interpretation of this moment is in the *Cumbrian Railway Photographer*. Swansea Victoria lost all its services in 1964/65 with the re-routing of Central Wales trains at Pontardulais onto the GWR via Llanelli. The prominent hill in the background is the 632 ft-high Kilvey Hill beneath which the rival Midland had made its way into town.

The exit from Victoria involved quite a pull which both these photographs show. The South Dock is over to the right out of sight and somewhere right of middle of the photo, there was a physical connection, which joined the Great Western and Midland systems with the LNWR through the dockland, the so-called Swansea High Level Lines. The Victoria terminus is tucked away out of sight behind the large building in the centre, which was a goods shed. The area is now a leisure centre. Near to Victoria was the Rutland Street terminus of the Swansea and Mumbles Railway whose origins went back to 1804. Swansea had another two termini (St Thomas has already been seen) to make a total of five: the surviving High Street of the Great Western; and Riverside of the Rhondda & Swansea Bay Railway. The Swansea and Mumbles is affectionately remembered having closed in 1960. Very careful inspection of the picture (beneath the loading gauge) enables one to spot the poles for the tramway overhead, for in 1929 the line was electrified and huge 106-seat tramcars introduced. The roof of one of these can be made out. Swansea in 1934 was intensely interesting to any railway enthusiast.

This April 1934 sequence moves north up the Central Wales Line, the bulk of which remains open including Pontardulais. This was the key junction heading south into Swansea, the view looks north to Llandeilo. It may remain open but it has been extremely rationalised, there is no signalling or pointwork left at all. The station was hard by the tidal head of the River Loughor and to the north the hills crowded in, the easier land to the south allowing LNWR (*right*) and GWR (*left*) routes to split and run either side of the estuary. An ex-LNWR engine is shunting. The coaching stock was noted by Nash as the 12.15 pm LMS local from Swansea Victoria. The signalling and the box are pure Great Western.

North of Pontadulais to Llandeilo the Central Wales route was entirely Great Western track, whereupon it became a joint GWR/LNWR (or LMS) line to Llandovery, before being exclusively LNWR onwards to Craven Arms, whence more joint GWR/LNWR track ran into Shrewsbury. This is relevant preamble because, in the LNWR's drive to South West Wales, Llandeilo marked a junction. The better known route went to Swansea but from 1871 the LNWR had its own route further west, from Llandeilo to Carmarthen. This would close entirely in 1963 but along the way, at Nantgaredig, Nash photographed in April 1934 the 4.46 pm Fish from Carmarthen to Crewe. The single line staff is in the process of being exchanged so the train appears to be running through non-stop. The engine was an ex-LNWR 2-4-2T No. 6740.

This is a selection from these April 1934 images, which also include Llandeilo Bridge, Llandeilo and Llandovery. Whenever Nash reached Llanwrtyd Wells it was pouring. All the atmosphere of the inter-war railway is there, canopies, signs, barrows, water column, posters, the named station seat, footbridge, gas lamps (surely?). Something does survive of this scene for the station is still a passing place on the Central Wales.

At Knighton, Nash took a characterful picture of the station and goods yard, one of the key notes being the prominent LNWR design of lower quadrant signals. Knighton's station buildings had a French feel to them. Knighton town is in Wales but all but a few square feet of the station are in England. A small signal box can be seen at the end of the station building. There is no signal box now but in Nash's time (and into the 1960s) this was 'Knighton No. 2'. Immediately behind Nash's vantage point was a substantial stone goods shed.

Our final view from this wayside selection is of Hopton Heath, last but one stop before the main line was regained at Craven Arms. Hopton Heath has in one respect not changed at all. It is still open to passengers and nestling in the sleepy Clun Valley must have been then, as now, one of the quieter spots of the railway network. Even so, Nash could find a bevy of wagons, including some three-plank wagons for stone traffic. B.Q.C was the British Quarrying Company. Modellers are familiar with these pale red wagons through the Peco Wonderful Wagon kit made in the 1960s. Nash completed his coverage of the Central Wales line with a picture of the final station at Broome. There and at Hopton Heath, he was on his way back to Crewe and it is back to Crewe that Nash's career went on 21st April, 1934; this series of April 1934 photos of the route up from Swansea Victoria seem a valediction to his time in South Wales. The chapter after next will return to his career, but meanwhile, it's time for some gallivanting . . .

Chapter Nine

Busman's Holidays by Bike

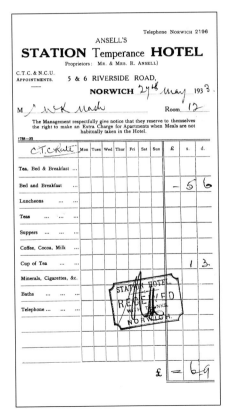

During the 1930s Nash continued to travel and this chapter draws upon excursions which appear 'beyond work'. These were latterly undertaken with his wife Marjory. Nash had married in Crewe in 1934, their acquaintance went back to his time at Carnforth, for she was the daughter of the Assistant Postmaster there. Early married life must have been quite taxing as Nash was also looking after his mother Ida who died in 1936.

Nash was a keen cyclist who often would cycle 50 miles for a day's outing. Each summer between 1932 and 1938 (save 1936), he went on a cycling holiday using Cyclist Touring Club materials for planning (*overleaf*). From 1935 his wife Marjory accompanied him. Each of these holidays is meticulously recorded with postcards, receipts, gradient profiles and mile logs surviving. The postcard illustrated below was sent on the 1932 trip, the view depicted on the reverse was a near identical scene to that illustrated on page 143 from Nash's own camera, and it is the postcard referred to in that caption.

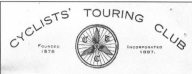

CYCLISTS' TOURING CLUB

Founded 1878 — Incorporated 1887.

Telegrams: "Cosmopolitan," Padd., London. Telephone: Paddington 8971/2.

Headquarters :
3, Craven Hill, Paddington, London, W.2.

ROUTE CARD.

STAGES	MILES	TOTAL
MACCLESFIELD		
BUXTON	10	
Forward by A.6 to		
ASHFORD	10	
Left fork on leaving. Under railway at $1\frac{1}{2}$ miles. Cross A.622 at crossroads in a further $\frac{1}{2}$ mile. Join A.619 in a further $\frac{3}{4}$ mile, turning left and taking Left fork to		
BASLOW	$4\frac{3}{4}$	
C.13		
CHESTERFIELD	$8\frac{1}{2}$	
Straight on by A.619		
STAVELEY	4	
Straight on by A.619 via Barlborough Whitwell to		
WORKSOP	11	
Forward by A.57, turning Right at $1\frac{1}{2}$ miles - A.57. Straight on over crossroads by A.57 to Elkesley and junction with A.1 at		
MARKHAM MOOR INN	10	
Forward by A.1, and Left at fork to		
EAST MARKHAM	$1\frac{1}{2}$	

CYCLISTS' TOURING CLUB

Founded 1878 — Incorporated 1887.

Telegrams: "Cosmopolitan," Padd., London. Telephone: Paddington 8971/2.

Headquarters :
3, Craven Hill, Paddington, London, W.2.

ROUTE CARD.

STAGES	MILES	TOTAL
Forward by A.57 via Darlton and Newton on Trent to		
SAXILBY	$10\frac{1}{2}$	
Straight on by A.57 to		
LINCOLN	6	
Forward by A.157 to		
WRAGBY	11	
Right fork on leaving by A.158 to		
HORNCASTLE	9	
Leave by A.153. Left fork at 1 mile to		
MOORBY	$4\frac{1}{2}$	
Continue by main road. Over crossroads and straight on at		
REVESBY	$2\frac{1}{2}$	
Frithville		
BOSTON	12	
A.16		
SUTTERTON	$6\frac{1}{4}$	
A.17		
KINGS LYNN	$28\frac{1}{2}$	
Tour No. 9		
CROMER	$65\frac{1}{4}$	
A.147		

CYCLISTS' TOURING CLUB

Founded 1878 — Incorporated 1887.

Telegrams: "Cosmopolitan," Padd., London. Telephone: Paddington 8971/2.

Headquarters :
3, Craven Hill, Paddington, London, W.2.

ROUTE CARD.

STAGES	MILES	TOTAL
AYLSHAM	$10\frac{1}{2}$	
Turn Right by B.1145		
CAWSTON	5	
REEPHAM	-	
BAWDESWELL	6	
B.1145		
NORTH ELMHAM	4	
Left to		
EAST DEREHAM	5	
Left by A.47 to		
HONINGHAM	8	
Straight on to		
NORWICH	8	
		~~36~~
		$261\frac{3}{4}$

On 10th September, 1932 Nash was at York as part of a York to Carnforth tour. All three railway pictures he made that day are reproduced. They are very expressive of the character of that large railway station in the 1930s. The first image is of No. 4475 *Flying Fox* one of the Gresley Pacific engines immortalised by No. 4472 *Flying Scotsman*. The train was noted as the 12.10 pm Glasgow to York. *Flying Fox* might have excited Nash's attention because she had been one of the LNER's contenders in the 1925 locomotive exchanges being put up against the GWR's *Pendennis Castle*. Unfortunately No. 4475 ran a hot box. In Nash's picture her original tender has been replaced, probably by a corridor-fitted version. A Nash view of No. 4475 in her original condition at Grantham is in Chapter Three. The lower quadrant semaphore signalling in the picture is original North Eastern Railway; note the arms working in each direction on the one post.

The tank engine No. 399, whose typical duty would have been as station pilot, came from class 'J71'. These, along with the slightly larger 'J72' (once NER 'E' and 'E1' respectively) were Victorian designs from the hand of T.W. Worsdell. With well over 200 in traffic and a building span between 1886 and 1951, they were ubiquitious on the former NER lines and one of the 'J72s' survives in preservation.

The third image shows another Pacific engine, named *City of Durham*. This was not one of the Gresley Pacifics but came from the rival North Eastern Railway in the year before Grouping. As a result only five of these Raven-designed 'A2' class engines were built between 1922-24 and all had gone by 1937. LNER No. 2403 was noted as hauling the 10.25 am Aberdeen to London Kings Cross. The York images form the lead into this small group known to come from September 1932 and which cover a tour of the former NER. The locations reached on this trip included York, Malton, Pickering, Barnard Castle and Alston.

At Malton station on 12th September, 1932 Nash found a former NER 2-4-2T, engine No. 1580 of class 'F8'. His own recording went astray as his notebook turns it into an 0-4-4T, he must have thought it was one of the 'G5s'. That class lasted until 1958 whilst the smaller number of 'F8s' were all gone by 1938. As Nash also photographed the 6.40 am York to Scarborough parcels (next in his sequence), his confusion is excusable. A card to his mother says 'Called at Malton station before breakfast this morning. Malton dep 9.44 . . .' The three horseboxes in the background might perhaps be linked to nearby Castle Howard? Not necessarily, as Malton station was the focus for a number of local racing stables and in 1913, incredibly, dispatched 4,971 tons of manure. The LNER invested in a series of motor horseboxes to connect the station to the stables. Local trains were already starting to be withdrawn in the 1930s and one of the services from Malton, that to Gilling, lost its stopping trains in 1931.

Nash managed to 'cop' the shed at Malton in the low morning light. At least four engines are on shed. Those identified by Nash were LNER Nos. 831 and 171. No. 831 is the straightforward 'J26' 0-6-0 on the right, in 1933 only one engine of this class was allocated, from a total of 18. No. 171 on the left is more interesting, again it was the only engine of its type at Malton. It was from class 'Y1', the LNER's classification for 53 (including the similar 'Y3') Sentinel four-wheeled shunters that the company invested in from 1925. These were innovative with a vertical boiler and chain drive. This engine was new in 1929 and lasted until 1952, many (all?) of those years being spent at Malton. Renumbered 8147 in 1946, it was still at Malton at Nationalisation. Malton shed shut on the 13th April, 1963. Not a trace is left although the 1845 station is still open.

Pickering station was next to be visited. Here is a scene which thanks to the North Yorkshire Moors Railway can still be recognised. Sadly none of the Worsdell 'G5' 0-4-4T engines made it into preservation. No. 505 was entering the station from the north with the 10.05 am Whitby to Malton. Trains were generally extended to York only in the summer season. The stock consists of NER clerestory coaches. The enamel station sign to the right is from the NER era and would have been in chocolate-orange and cream. Pickering had been the original terminus of the line from Whitby, which opened in 1837, before the extension to Malton opened in 1845. Currently Pickering is the terminus again, although there is a lobby to re-open the connection to Malton lost in 1965. Out of sight behind the photographer was the station designed by G.T. Andrews who did so much railway work in Yorkshire. His design included an overall roof, which Nash would have seen. This was removed in 1951.

Nash went on from Pickering to Whitby for the night, cycling over the moors. His camera was used for plenty of non-railway subjects on these holidays although, in this image, the railway does feature. This is the Whitby to Pickering line now part of the North Yorkshire Moors Railway. Nash hedged his bets, the same view is in the postcard that he sent to his office mates, signing himself B for Bill as he was known in the office. The picture looks down the Eller Beck towards Goathland in the distance with the railwaymen's cottages, now long demolished, at Fen Bog in the middle of the image.

This print is full of the atmosphere of the 1930s railway. Is there the whiff of roses to the right? The lattice post signals and gantry with spiky finials are wonderfully North Eastern Railway; however as a result of the 1923 Grouping, the engine is ex-Great Northern Railway (south of Doncaster). Such was Barnard Castle on 14th September, 1932 as the 5.15 pm Bishop Auckland to Middleton-in-Teesdale went past the town's small engine shed: roses, coal and steam. The shed was closed in 1937 and the railway in 1964. Engine No. 4077 was one of six 'D3' class engines brought north in 1930/31 where they did not prove terribly popular. One of the bulky NER carriages shows off a clerestory roof whilst the front vehicle has a 'birdcage' lookout in the roof for the guard. Nash wrote, 'The stationmaster at Barnard Castle was most kind and showed me all over the place'. Nash's September 1932 journey headed on from Barnard Castle over Yad Moss at the head of Teesdale to Alston, with prints there reproduced in *Cumbrian Railway Photographer*.

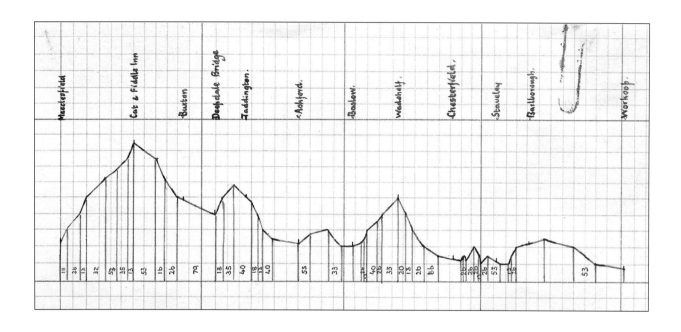

Section of gradient profile prepared by William Nash before his summer cycle tour of 1933.

Nash found himself at Dereham in Norfolk during his May 1933 cycle tour from Macclesfield to Norwich. This was a holiday taken the week before his move to Swansea as District Runner. Taken on 26th May, 1933, it was the only railway photograph from that year, apart from one of posters at Swansea printed in *Cumbrian Railway Photographer*. The engine is LNER No. 7415, an 'E4' class 2-4-0 originally designed by Holden for the Great Eastern Railway as its No. 415. Its life between 1902-37 was relatively short. The class were the last 2-4-0 engines at work in mainland Britain. Former GER No. 490 lasted until 1960 before being preserved. Dereham shed had been home to several of the class until the mid-1950s. The GER dominated East Anglia, it would take-over the lines that had previously, from 1847, opened to Dereham . Despite a steady rundown since 1964, the rails never left Dereham and, in recent years, the line to Wymondham and thus the national network has re-opened. The train is heading north from Dereham and this would suggest it is either a Wells-bound passenger train or a working for Norwich via County School and Aylsham. The corner of Dereham North signal box intrudes at the left-hand side. Nash was likely to have taken his photograph by jamming himself up against the level crossing gates of Norwich Road. A station lamp hides the Hobbies lettering. This company was for decades Dereham's largest employer and a good customer of the railway. They specialised in wooden fretwork kits. The company had started out in 1895 by publishing *Hobbies*, a weekly journal, from an old carriage at the station.

At an earlier stage in his life, Southern Railway subjects had been popular with Nash but they were uncommon in the 1930s save for a small group taken at Exeter in March 1936. Two are reproduced here. The interest in this image of Exeter Central station is coupled behind the ex-LSWR 'G6' 0-6-0T No. 237. It is a bogie goods brake van, a concept always rare in Britain but developed to some extent on the Southern Railway. Yet this vehicle is not one of the 1936 purpose-built 'Queen Mary' brake vans. It is even more interesting for it is a 1934 rebuild of an electric locomotive! The origins are revealed by its sheet steel panelling and ducket layout. What started the Southern down the bogie brake line was the need to do something useful with the redundant components of some 1925-built Motor Luggage Vans, originally built for an overhead line electrified project of the former London Brighton & South Coast Railway. As such these vehicles only worked for four years. This batch of 21 brakes then led a useful life until 1955-57. As for the 'G6', No. 237 was in action from 1898-1949. It was one of a workaday class of 34. That 1949 withdrawal put it amongst the first of the class to go, extinction did not come until 1962.

Rather more central to the subject was the Southern's investment in the very useful Moguls that had started with the Maunsell 'N' class in 1917 and continued until 1934. Southern No. 1840 was one of these, bought after the Grouping having been built at Woolwich Arsenal for unemployment relief purposes. The train is the 11.46 am to Ilfracombe and the picture was taken down the fearsome bank from the Southern's Central station at the Great Western's St David's station.

Nash took three holidays in Scotland in the 1930s. These visited some attractive locations and the selection follows his order commencing with those from a holiday undertaken in May 1934. First off is a view of Newton Stewart on 29th May, 1934 with a morning train to Whithorn leaving behind LMS No. 17421. This was one of the large number of 'Jumbo' or '2F' 0-6-0s that the Caledonian Railway had contributed to the LMS in 1923. Examples worked the branch from Newton Stewart for decades. By 1934 this was pure LMS territory, but, before 1923, the railways of Newton Stewart had been part of the Portpatrick and Wigtownshire Joint with four owning partners. The view looks east with the junction behind the camera. The branch train will need to cross the layout to gain the branch. The photo is taken from the B7051 road overbridge which offered a vantage point. The two layers of hill beyond the town on the other side of the Cree Valley (left of the steam) are Larg Hill and Cairnsmore of Fleet, the latter rising to 2,331 ft. The railway closed here in 1965. Nash reached Newton Stewart by cycling the twisty road from Girvan, a card to mum says: 'Yesterday I carefully left my camera behind at Girvan incurring about seventeen miles extra'.

Working back from Wigtownshire, Nash put the Moniaive branch in rural Dumfriesshire on his agenda. Here he had the full co-operation of the station master with whom he stayed the night of the 29th/30th May, 1934. This is the view looking to Moniaive's deserted terminus. The little wooden station building remained when one of the authors passed by in the late 1990s. It had not seen a railway for about 50 years, goods services went in 1947.

The passenger trains had gone in 1943 which makes this image all the more interesting. The branch, which had only opened in 1905, had been promoted as the Cairn Valley Light Railway, a technical procedure which made economies possible. Despite which, it was essentially a failure. Crossford, 14 miles out from Dumfries, was the second to last station. Former Caledonian Railway 'Jumbo' now LMS No. 17339, had taken over on this erstwhile Glasgow & South Western Railway branch by May 1934. The 9.48 am from Moniaive to Dumfries had just a couple of coaches as it rolled into the station. The angle of the fence (*bottom right*) suggests Nash's vantage point was the platform end.

The 10 am Euston to Glasgow 'Royal Scot' approaches Beattock station from the south. The train engine is a 'Royal Scot' class engine, No. 6156 *The South Wales Borderer*. The 14-carriage train appears to be mostly modern Stanier steel-sided coaching stock. Nash wrote in his daily card to his mother: 'The stationmaster at Beattock entertained me to an excellent tea, and we talked for nearly two hours'.

Not for Nash the detailed recording of the expresses tackling Beattock; after his one main line picture, it was a visit to the short branch line to Moffat from Beattock. This was the scene at the terminus in May 1934. One coach sufficed for the job, the passenger service here was withdrawn in 1954. The engine LMS No. 15239 was quite modern having been built in 1922 as Caledonian Railway No. 433. In origin the design dated back to 1900 but the 1922 engines were more powerful and incorporated a cast-iron buffer beam for use as a banking engine. Beattock shed used these engines for that task on the famous Beattock Bank. The spruced-up condition of the locomotive is noteworthy - look at those bufferheads and other brightwork.

The ex-Caledonian 0-4-4Ts on the Moffat branch were sufficiently interesting to Nash that he photographed another working approaching the terminus on or around the same day in May 1934. This time the engine was No. 15164, one of the rather earlier and much more numerous build from the Edwardian era, without the banker fitments of the previous engine.

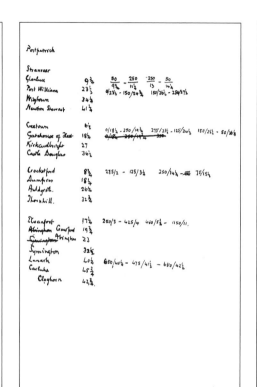

Is this an LMS handbill for an excursion to the FA cup final from Crewe or William's log of his cycle tour a month later?

The final group of three holiday pictures all revolve around the branch line to Kyle of Lochalsh. Nash and his wife made two holidays in successive years to the north-west Highlands and amongst his general portrayal of those holidays were three rail-related subjects. Nash took very few (if any other?) shipping pictures but the presence of the TSMV *Lochnevis* at Kyle of Lochalsh did attract his camera in June 1937. Her interest was that she was the second diesel-electric ship built for MacBraynes. Entering service in 1934, she would have appeared very modern in 1937. She had been designed for year-round use on the mail service from Mallaig-Kyle-Portree. Her life with MacBraynes lasted until 1970. They were a partly rail-owned company.

Nash got to the Kyle line in the last years before the standard LMS designs, most noticeably the 'Black 5' 4-6-0 took over. Instead he managed two pictures of a small class of eight 4-6-0 engines built for the Highland Railway and tucked in virtually at the end of the LMS numbering system. At Kyle of Lochalsh in June 1937 was LMS No. 17955. The engines were from the 'Clan Goods' class with smallish 5 ft 3 in. driving wheels. This one had been Highland Railway No. 80 built in 1919.

Next year in May 1938, Nash was at Achnasheen, the principal intermediate passing station on the line. There he photographed No. 17957 bringing the 10.15 am Inverness to Kyle into the station. This engine was one of two of the class which did not make it into BR days, being withdrawn in 1946.

Chapter Ten

Innovation in Reports

At the start of Chapter Seven, William Nash's CV was reproduced. Precisely why he produced it is not known and it is not dated. At the bottom he had added some handwritten information. This gives further positions that he had held between 1933 and 1936, after which we don't have any access to the remaining 16 years of his railway career in that medium.

His progress had been rapid. In Swansea he had been District Runner until his move back to Crewe in 1934 as Passenger Train Inspector.

The last entry is the meat of this chapter. He notes that from 29th September, 1936, he was Electrification Clerk, Commercial Department in the Euston Headquarters of the LMS. Writing a letter to a friend from Swansea, in 1940, Nash says: 'In May 1936 I was made a passenger trains clerk in the Chief Commercial Manager's offices at Euston House, and in a reorganisation in the following September I was virtually given charge of electrification schemes and London Transport matters'. Buried in Nash's materials are the outputs of that position and they are not likely to be widely known. Nash it seems was given the job of compiling three significant reports (at least, judging by surviving copies), a task at which he worked for about three years.

The first of these was *The Commercial Possibilities of Electrifying the Midland Division Main Line Between London and Harpenden* which is dated September 1938.

One intriguing comment in this 1938 report reveals that back in 1930 the LMS had prepared paperwork for an electrification scheme to Harpenden. Indeed the 1940 report with which this chapter concludes refers to three schemes that the LMS completed, to examinations of the electrification of both the West Coast and Midland Main Lines and to 11 potential suburban schemes.

When electrification finally reached the Midland line, it was with a 25,000v AC scheme undertaken between 1976 and 1983. It took the wires to Bedford beyond Harpenden and at Bedford in the world of the privatised railway, they remain.

One of the tasks Nash undertook was to estimate likely traffic and housing growth if the scheme was adopted. As a result he got his camera out to illustrate the line. He illustrated the report with seven pictures, three of which are reproduced. The first of which was labelled 'Medburn looking south' (*overleaf*). A local train is approaching. This is north of Elstree and Nash's report considered the merits of a station there. None was ever to appear.

Parkbury was the location for a suggested station by Nash. The print was labelled 'Parkbury looking south-west'. Parkbury is north of Radlett near Colney Street. Nash's understanding of the planning process evidently led him to think the station could form the nucleus of a new settlement here. No station is here in 2003.

The last choice was taken near Harpenden Common. Development was taking place. The notice by the line starts 'Grange Estate Harpenden Common Homes of Distinction'. This had been proposed as a station in the 1930 Electrification Scheme. This is another of the several (there are more) locations where the LMS was considering new stations on the line to Harpenden and where over the decades no new stations have appeared. One angle where the project became bogged down was in its relationship to the London Transport scheme which electrified the LNER branch to Edgware as far as Mill Hill East but never, owing to the war, reached the Midland Main Line at Mill Hill Broadway, let alone Edgware and Elstree/Bushey (it's there on a 1946 LT journey planner). Nash could see merit in a junction and not just a flyover there, and some planning for this junction with the LMS was undertaken. Not only did the war intervene but a key minute was referred to by Nash in which it had been agreed that the LMS scheme would not be progressed until LT had experience of its own extension to Elstree, a project which was not then and never has been completed. It was not only the war that frustrated these schemes for LMS and LT development but after the war the advent of the Green Belt discouraged the building that would have provided the traffic.

Next in the sequence is *Electrification and the LMS Railway* of August 1939. Although the Southern Railway was the leader in this technology among the 'Big Four', the LMS was far from disinterested and Nash reviewed the experience of nine local areas where the LMS used electric traction, all for suburban passenger traffic. It is evident that the report was written directly for the company Chairman and one of its conclusions was that not all was rosy. In essence it could be shown in the inter-war climate that electrification could stimulate housing development and the local economy but that growth did not necessarily flow straight back to the LMS, indeed bus operators could be the beneficiaries. In crystal gazing Nash concluded that Birmingham, whilst apparently a candidate for electrification was a very complex situation, and that his preferred target was the Manchester, Hazel Grove and Alderley Edge group of services, something that did take place roughly 20 years on. Nash was also working on the obvious main line scheme for the West Coast route and a lot of background research was evidently done before 1939. He had been diverted into a partial scheme for the London-Rugby route and was evidently not impressed by that idea. In 2003 of the main line destinations he mentioned, Blackpool remains without wires. His angle is interesting in that these are not technical reports on which system to use but commercial reports about how the business of the company might be affected. Nowadays they would probably not be regarded as sufficiently statistical.

The Alderley Edge scheme did become part of the Manchester/Crewe/Liverpool electrification of the late 1950s. By then the technical parameters of the scheme had changed from 1,500v. DC to 25,000v. AC (both with overhead wires). Allowing for the intervention of World War II, this August 1939 report (*right*) that he was evidently preparing, in parallel to the broader report just described, was not wasted work. Nash had had to learn shorthand when he had entered LMS service and the surviving copy of his report has his shorthand pages in neat green ink affixed at the rear. The Alderley Edge report is about 40 pages and Nash was optimistic that the stations were well located for future development and that if the scheme went ahead, the LMS would profit. After five years, he estimated that the lines would generate an additional £50,000 of traffic. He envisaged the scheme as an extension of the already electrified Manchester to Altrincham route and he proposed that the Buxton line as far as Hazel Grove should be electrified. All this has happened, the last element to Hazel Grove being completed in 1981. Owing to the change in traction voltage, it was not until 1971 that the through trains to Altrincham operated.

THE COMMERCIAL POSSIBILITIES OF

THE ELECTRIFICATION OF THE

MANCHESTER, HAZEL GROVE, AND

ALDERLEY EDGE SECTION.

Chief Commercial Manager's Office,
Passenger Revenue Section,
EUSTON.
(BP 3/407.7. 10.8.39)

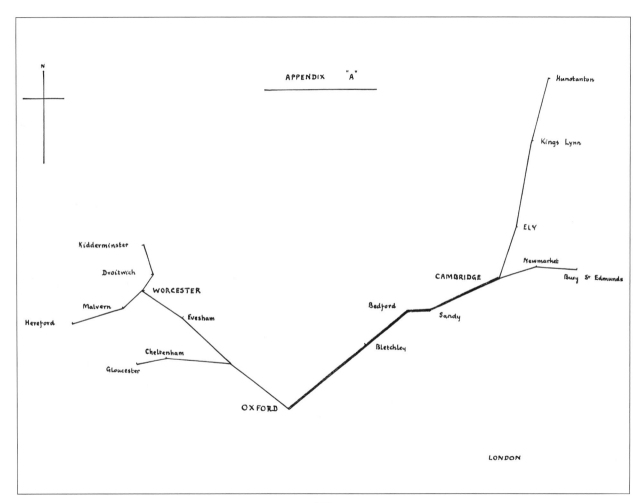

APPENDIX "A"

N

Hunstanton

Kings Lynn

ELY

Kidderminster

Droitwich

WORCESTER

Newmarket

CAMBRIDGE

Bury St Edmunds

Malvern

Evesham

Hereford

Bedford

Sandy

Cheltenham

Bletchley

Gloucester

OXFORD

LONDON

164

BPH/W.Spring.

Passenger Revenue Section.
Euston.

July, 1936.

Memorandum to

Employment of 3-coach Diesel Trains.
Oxford and Cambridge Section.

The choice of the section between Oxford and Cambridge for the trials of the 3-coach Diesel trains, is a happy one for mechanical reasons, and because the introduction of an improved service will render possible a test of the statements so frequently made, that the public would respond eagerly to the provision of better facilities between these points. It is very improbable, however, that express traffic originating in and between Oxford and Cambridge, would come near to paying for augmented train-mileage, and it is therefore incumbent upon the Passenger Revenue Section to consider whether the public usefulness of the service can be increased, and whether any other streams of traffic can be diverted into the new channel. It is the purpose of this memorandum to indicate a plan of service which will achieve this end.

Evidently the new service cannot cater for local as well as for end-to-end traffic, apart from Bletchley, Bedford, and Sandy, because an attempt to do so would at once rob it of its express character, on which it will largely depend for its success; but it could be made an attractive link between the G.W Worcester Division and the Ely area of the G.E section, L.& N.E.R, while still providing for the needs of traffic to originate at Oxford and Cambridge. A measure of the potential increase in the utility of the new route may be obtained from a statement of the populations of the principal towns in the areas in which the new service would show to advantage. They are:

OXFORD	81,000	CAMBRIDGE	67,000
Evesham	11,000		
Worcester	50,000	Newmarket	10,000
Droitwich	5,000	Bury St Edmunds	17,000
Kidderminster	29,000	Ely	8,000
Malvern	16,000	Kings Lynn	21,000
Hereford	24,000	Hunstanton	3,000
Cheltenham	49,000		
Gloucester	53,000		

This is very encouraging, and suggests that suitable drafting of the service will multiply its usefulness some six-fold.

Not all Nash's report work involved electrification. Two more significant pre-1940 reports sit in the trunk. A memorandum with his signature from July 1936 (before becoming an Electrification clerk) is headed *Employment of 3-coach Diesel Trains Oxford and Cambridge Section*. This is extremely interesting for it shows Nash to have been involved in the planning of an innovation that was followed through, even if the war, again, brought the investment to a stop.

Nash evidently felt that the introduction of an express diesel train to the route was a good choice but that the extent of the market for express travel solely along the Oxford-Cambridge channel was limited. At the time he may have been correct, although nowadays things may be different. What will not have changed however is the potential role of the route in a chain between Hunstanton, Lynn, Ely and onwards from Oxford to the towns of the Severn Valley like Gloucester and Worcester. To that end he conceived a clever timetable to make these connections (see reproduced map) and a complete working timetable for all envisaged services on the Oxford-Cambridge run. A journey from Ely to Malvern would change from 5½ hours to 4. He emphasised potential growth of market as six fold and (correctly) advocated that the new train required successful and targeted marketing. He also appreciated that the pooling arrangements between different companies might mitigate some of the hoped-for benefits.

This train was completed in January 1938. It went into service on the Oxford-Cambridge route in September 1938. The timetable was not precisely as Nash envisaged and nor is it clear that it was the commercial success he had hoped, but was it 'sold' the way he suggested? Having worked this line for some months, it was used on the Midland Main Line before it was stored during the war, after which this unique train suffered the ignominy of being converted into an overhead line maintenance unit for use in the Manchester area, last being noted derelict in 1967. Would that Nash had photographed it! Instead from one of the authors' collections, this postcard showing train Nos. 80000-2 when brand new is reproduced. Its streamlined nature, articulated as three components, appealed to the climate of the times. More than a decade after the war, diesel trains were introduced between the Varsity towns in 1959, after a 1955 report that foresaw a rosy future for this route linking five main lines. Instead all but Bedford to Bletchley was closed to passengers at the start of 1968. Much of the route remained intact and local trains have returned on the Oxford-Bicester stretch. Plans to re-open the route continue to be mooted and the Oxford-Cambridge railway must be one of the best examples of an unnecessary closure of the 1960s. *R.N. Forsythe Collection*

**PROGRESS AND DEVELOPMENTS
IN THE
CHIEF OPERATING MANAGER'S DEPARTMENT
IN THE
YEARS PRIOR TO THE WAR**

Chief Operating Manager's Office,
WATFORD   *February, 1940*

Throughout the second part of the 1930s, the gathering storm clouds of war grew. Nash, a committed Christian and an international correspondent (*see next chapter*) was fully aware of all this.

When the storm broke and it was evident that war would be a long haul, a degree of stocktaking and farewells to the old order evidently took place. During the period of the phoney war, officials of the LMS (we assume including Nash) were able to prepare an 82 page fully printed analysis of their achievements. Think of it: these gentleman wanted to preserve something in print of what they had done in the face of an oncoming Armageddon that guaranteed none of them survival.

T.W. Royle (to whom the diesel report was addressed) is the signatory of this report although one guesses Nash had had some role in it. Royle's own understated words from the Foreword are worth quoting '. . . an attempt to . . picture . . . the high spots of Railway Operating policy . . . since . . . the setting up of a Chief Operating Manager's Department . . . that should the War last . . . it will be possible at its termination . . . to pick up the threads of the various activities and carry them forward to a successful conclusion even if some of the Officers and Staff of the Operating Department . . . are no longer available'.

The result is a kaleidoscopic review with such headings as 'Introduction of Camping Coaches', 'Light units, Push and Pull Trains', a whole section (XI) on 'Electrification Schemes', two from the 'Miscellaneous Items' headings are 'Closing of branch lines' and 'Education of staff through the medium of Cinematograph Films'. Its 82 pages form a review of the company operations both in detail and in broad theme.

With this, the demands of war took over. The railways would be subjected to a shock whose effect, in the denial of investment and the over-use of assets, would be felt for decades. Nash's own life was far from exempt and his copy of this report is marked 'Asst. Dist. Controller Rugby' at the top left of the cover.

168

Chapter Eleven

Esperanto and an International Dimension

There is nothing clever in those who mock 'railway enthusiasts' as anoraks. A pathetically pejorative term that thankfully Nash never had to endure. Nash was evidently proud to photograph and celebrate marvellous steam engines; that is the meat of this book. But he had become a railwayman, largely from outside the loop of the railway community. He understood from the outset that the railway did not exist for itself, it needed to be a successful business. Issues of marketing and technical innovation in the service of expanding the business interested him greatly. His religious faith ensured that the wider issues of the 1930s were not ignored in his own life.

He was a member of the Institute of Transport, the Railway Clerk's Association, the Cyclist's Touring Club, the Worker's Educational Association, the British Esperanto Association and the National Liberal Federation.

As the 1930s progressed, he corresponded at length with railwaymen in several continents. The results of this correspondence survive and produce some piquant images of the 1930s. Some of this is explored here, although it is stressed that none of the imagery shown in this chapter was originated by William Nash. Whilst at school he had learnt French, Latin, Greek and Spanish and in 1936 a relatively easy expansion saw him learn Esperanto and adopt its use with enthusiasm.

He was known to advise school leavers who desired a railway career to learn shorthand BEFORE joining the railway since learning both shorthand and block signalling rules at the same time was not recommended. He also advised these gentlemen to learn Spanish because the British owned the railways of South America.

Nash had corresponded in the mid-1930s with first a Spaniard and subsequently a German. Those pen friendships did not last, despite spending six guineas with Linguaphone on a set of Spanish records - still owned by the family, whereas his 1936 adoption of Esperanto did. When the Spanish correspondence ceased during the Spanish Civil War, Nash undertook to learn German and swapped political ideas: 'Kurt has sent me an English translation of a speech by Dr. Goebbels which looks like propaganda . . .' (21st May, 1936).

Esperanto had been launched in 1887 by a 28-year-old Polish Jew, Ludovic Zamenhof. He intended it as a means of reconciliation for communities riven by ethnic strife, although Hitler described it as 'a tool of Jewish world domination'. It was proposed as the language of the League of Nations, whereupon the French banned it from their schools.

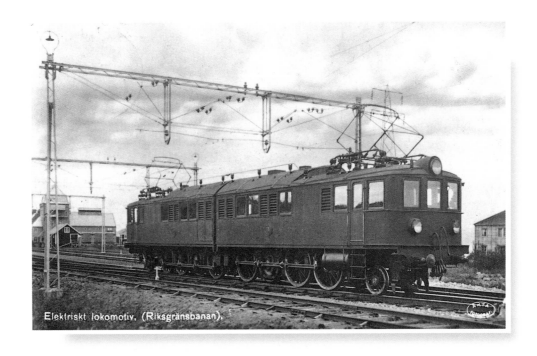

Elektriskt lokomotiv, (Riksgränsbanan).

In a 1940 letter Nash listed 13 countries to which he corresponded in Esperanto including Brazil, Russia, Czechoslovakia and Finland. He said about half his correspondents were railwaymen and that by 1940 he had spent three years as the railway representative of the Esperanto movement. He sadly stated that 'most of this has been interrupted by the German invasion(s)'. Scandinavia was well represented and this postcard came from a gentleman who would prove long lasting as a correspondent, one Hermann Nordling. It was sent in 1937 and represented an electric locomotive of 1,600hp and 1-C+C-1 layout built by Asea/Siemens-Schuckert from 1911. This was engine No. 75 for a 120 kilometre line in Lapland, the Riksgränsbanan which translates into Frontier Railway. Heavy iron ore trains formed part of the incentive behind adopting the new technology which might have looked radical to the Englishman in 1937 but was well established to this Swedish counterpart. The jackshaft drive used by this engine is evident. It was a principle widely used at the time when electric motors were still relatively large pieces of machinery.

One of the photographs sent to Nash was a delightful view of this wayside Swedish station called Billesholm. This is a small junction between Halmstad and Teckomatorp some way south of the Lapland system of the previous card and on the Swedish 'West Coast' route. The line has been electrified from the 1st December, 1934 although the little engine is a Swedish State Railways four-wheeled diesel shunter No. 55. This is a 150 hp Z49 shunter made in 1935. This engine is preserved. Whilst the LMS was a bit ambivalent about electrification in practice, it and thereby Nash did accept the role of the diesel as an effective shunting unit.

Elektriskt lok littra M, vid SJ.

Hermann Nordling was a correspondent from the 1930s into the 1950s, one portrait of this gentleman is annotated in Nash's hand 'Christmas 1951'. This is a post-war card with Hermann's stamp on the back and details typed in Esperanto. The engine was another with Asea equipment, one of 17 supplied between 1944-5 to the SJ or Swedish State Railways. It is a Litra M (class 'M') Co-Co with all wheels motored and individually driven hollow axles which proved not to be tough enough in service when applied to this forward thinking design. Engine No. 604 in the picture was the class leader and worked until the mid-1970s, one example of the class was preserved.

This gentleman looks like a French communist. He was, and a railway worker, called Henri Capiez. One of Henri's letters (from July 1937) includes these quotes 'for a long time I've thought that Christianity and Communism look the same, at least from the social side . . . Unfortunately the Catholic press don't play fair . . . every prudent worker aims to only live in peace and decency . . . our governments spend a lot of money (from our pockets, of course) to build up arms because of the doings of Hitler and his fellow war-mongers . . . excuse my poor writing – I'm more experienced with working a hammer than a pen'.

He lived in the railwaymen's housing at Valenciennes. His own house (of which he sent Nash photos) was a bit more modern than those in this postcard (which are visible in the Capiez prints). Valenciennes is an industrial centre near the Belgian border. After World War II, in the mid-1950s, the heavily used Valenciennes-Thionville line became a French success for 50-cycle AC traction. Judging by the postcards of electric traction that Nash's Esperanto colleagues sent him, this would have interested him greatly.

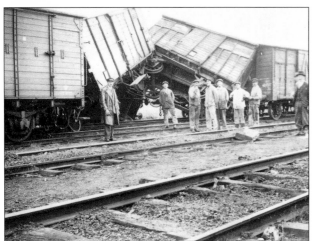

Left & Below left: Two of the images sent by Henri to William were of this scene of an accident in the Valenciennes area to a French Nord Railway goods train.

Below: The Eiffel Tower at night.

What do French communists do in World War II? They probably join the Resistance. Did Henri even get that chance? The last surviving letter was dated 22nd October, 1939.

Whilst some of the Esperanto correspondents surface after the war, nothing survives from Henri.

William Nash never visited Europe. His outer limits were Jersey and the Hebrides. When in 1937, the Paris Exposition was in the headlines, William did not go but Henri did, and sent him these pictures. The exhibition was centred around the Champ de Mars, the Eiffel Tower, the Pont d'Iéna and the Trocadéro. It became famous for the architects employed, and the sense of national rivalry foretelling the oncoming storm. This was exemplified by the display in the Spanish pavilion of Pablo Picasso's *Guernica*.

Above: The German pavilion whose architect was Albert Speer!

Right: The British pavilion (*left*) seen from the top of the German pavilion. The architect was Oliver Hill.

Inside the Soviet pavilion, whose architect was Boris Iofan, was this Soviet 2-8-4 engine.

The British Esperanto Association

(Incorporated)

Acting Secretary:
Cecil C. Goldsmith
— Telephone:
Chorley Wood 138
Telegrams:
Esperanto, Heronsgate
Rickmansworth

140, HOLLAND PARK AVE., LONDON, W.11.
Affiliated to Internacia Esperanto–Ligo.
Member of A.B.G.B.I.
War-time Address:
ESPERANTO HOUSE, HERONSGATE
RICKMANSWORTH, HERTS.

Secretary for Education,
Examinations
and Propaganda:
M. C. Butler, M.R.S.T.
36 Penrhyn Road
Kingston-on-Thames
Tel.: Kingston 1484

CCG/WWS.

19th January, 1943

S-ro W.K. Nash,
1, Southfield Road,
RUGBY, Wwks.

Dear Mr. Nash,

Thank you for your letter of the 17th. I am pleased to know that you hope to be present at the Council Meeting and if so you will then hear some very interesting figures.

I note what you state about standing for re-election and will read your letter to the Council. My own impression is that, in present circumstances, no changes will be made if that can be avoided. Council Meetings are nowadays comparatively few and your attendance as good as most people and better than some.

that of

Kind regards,

Yours sincerely,

Keith B Goldsmith

Acting Secretary.

Above: In 1938, the 30th Universal Esperanto Congress was held at University College, London. This postcard was produced specially printed in Esperanto. It is postally used with a 4th August, 1938 Esperanto frank, William sent it to himself. The address was Somerby (again), the house name William used for his Watford house. Nash wrote of the Congress: 'It was like a window into a future age, when mankind will have learnt that its enmities and wars are very great sins, and it will have become a real society'.

Left: Even in the war, Nash would continue Esperanto business. He was, after all, still present on the Home Front though as this letter shows the Nashes rented a house in Rugby (*see next chapter*). He was by then a member of Council for the British Esperanto Association whose head office was not so far from Nash's Watford home.

These pictures which are loose are something of a mystery. The limited information on the reverse in Esperanto reveals the date as 2nd May, 1944. The assumption must be that they show bomb damage 'somewhere in Europe' although how Nash came by them is not known.

December 17, 1937.

Dear Bill,

This doesn't count as a letter but is merely to let you know that we arrived safely on this side and that I am sending you under separate cover a slight memento of the many happy hours we spent with you and Marjorie. It is a paper weight model of one of our Hudson Type locomotives such as is used on our main line passenger service. The main engine develops a tractive effort of more than 43,000 pounds with an additional 12,000 pounds in the booster. The driving wheels are 79 inches in diameter. It is used in hauling trains of 1500 tons at speeds well over seventy miles an hour.

We had a good trip over. The first couple of days were a bit windy but after that it was very pleasant. The ship arrived in Boston about six thirty Sunday where we were met by my family. I spent Monday in Boston and then came down on the sleeper that night to New York. Virginia stayed in Boston where she will remain until after Christmas.

I find that I am not to be here after all. I was slated to go to Los Angeles as it was felt that it would be further good experience for me. However, now a job in Boston has opened up which is, aside from the personal preference of being near home, a better job. So now I am just waiting around to see which it will be. The boss is in Detroit at a meeting at which the head of the Boston area is as well and has taken my service record with him. So I am hopeful. I'll let you know where I land.

Please excuse the poor typing but I am doing it myself amid numerous interruptions and I'm not too good at best.

We both send our best to you and Marjorie.

As always,

Wallace Snow

Not all Nash's correspondence abroad was in Esperanto. A great friendship was made with an American, one Wally Snow and his wife.

The original link, however, for this friendship was Wally Snow's father, William Snow, who was a retired High School Principal from Boston, Massachusetts. William Snow and William Nash corresponded in Esperanto until the latter's wife died suddenly in the summer of 1938, after which he could often no longer summon up the extra effort to translate his thoughts into Esperanto, and resorted to writing mostly in English. The letters were searching and questioning, the international scene being uppermost on both sides of the Atlantic.

It seems amazing in today's world of English as the predominant world *lingua franca* that individuals in England, USA, Australia and New Zealand should *choose* to write to each other in a foreign language - but that is precisely what they did! William Nash corresponded with men in all of these places, although, during World War II, the Australian and New Zealand governments intervened and outlawed the use of Esperanto, presumably fearing subversive activities.

Wally Snow never learned Esperanto. The basis of his friendship with William Nash was railways. This was reinforced by a bond of friendship which grew up between the wives, lasting into the early 1960s. In 1937 Wally (with his wife) was sent by his employer, the New York Central System, to study British railway practice and William and his wife, Marjory, hosted them.

The letter on the previous page, on New York Central letterheaded paper was accompanied by a New York Central Hudson locomotive model paperweight. Wally sent William one of these which Kate Robinson continues to treasure.

In a quirk of fate, whilst in Britain the thunderclaps of war were about to start, Wally Snow took a promotion from 24th September, 1939. His move took him right across the Continent to San Francisco from Chicago. The day he started his new job, his wife was giving birth back in Chicago. No paternity leave then. Albeit the baby arrived early but as Snow noted, using the train, one day in Chicago required a week's leave from San Francisco. His new job entailed running an office dedicated to gaining as much traffic as he could to be routed over New York Central tracks from shippers originating in the West despite his employer's tracks being hundreds of mile away. To do it in 1940, New York Central gave him a company car with which he clocked up some 30,000 miles in the first year. In January 1941 Wally wrote to William: 'Mr Roosevelt has come out pretty strongly for all possible aid to you fellows . . . We are beginning to realise our own necks are at stake . . . it is expecting the superhuman for you to stand all Europe alone'. Wally and William were able to continue as friends despite the war when Wally, given the rank of Major in the Office of Chief of Transportation, was posted to London in the middle of 1942. His letters reveal vividly what it was to arrive in London and set up a new organisation from scratch. His job seems to have been responsible for moving incoming US supplies into and around Britain.

W. M. SNOW
GENERAL AGENT

G. M. McCORMICK
TRAVELING FREIGHT AGENT

C. J. BUTLER
TRAVELING FREIGHT AGENT

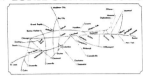

523 MONADNOCK BUILDING
TELEPHONE KEARNY 3682
SAN FRANCISCO

September 24, 1939.

Dear Bill;

I was very glad to hear from you, but I am equally sorry to learn that Marjory has had so much trouble. Here's hoping that it is all behind her now and that she soon will be feeling her normal self again. With world conditions as upset as they are now with the natural resultant strain it is particularly difficult to be under the weather at the same time.

As you have probably already heard from Virginia the new Snow arrived ahead of schedule on the 23rd of August, a boy who has been Wallace MacDonald, Jr. It so happened that I was transferred here to San Francisco and arrived the day the baby was born so that I have seen neither him nor his mother since the event. Had I realized that Don would arrive then I'ld have delayed leaving Chicago, but he wasn't due until around the fifteenth of September. Our people were quite anxious that I come out before my predecessor left so that he might show me about a little and gave me permission to return to Chicago to be present at the hospital. With the sudden arrival everything was over before I knew anything about it and as every one is doing well there is no real reason to make the trip which would require at least a week to be there only a day.

Virginia left the hospital some two weeks ago and is now in the apartment in Oak Park with a nurse awaiting the doctor's permission to go down to her family's who live about 150 miles from Chicago where she will stay until the doctors pronounce her sufficiently strong to undergo the long trip out here. As it takes three nights and two days constantly on the train without changing naturally they wish her to be as strong as possible. She will have a bedroom which will give her privacy and the train is completely air-conditioned so that she will not be bothered should the weather become hot. Also there is a stewardess on the train who is a trained nurse and who is supposed particularly to help mothers with babies and small children. Nevertheless it is a trip of over two thousand miles which is tiring even under the best conditions. She is hoping to join her family the latter part of this week and to start out here around the first of November. I shall probably meet her about half way.

The change out here was entirely unexpected. I took my annual leave the last two weeks in July the same as last year and joined my father in Maine. I hadn't been back at my desk an hour when my boss called me in and told me I was appointed out here the first of September and that he wanted me to leave to arrive a week or ten days ahead of that. At first I wasn't too pleased being transferred so far just at that time. However, as I thought it over it was a promotion and one can't be too choosy about rises or they cease to exist. Fortunately Virginia being the kind of a girl she is backed up my decision a hundred percent and said the only thing to do was to accept and go and that she would be all right. It must have taken a lot of spunk on her part but she stood up without a whimper or complaint. All she said was that she had always wanted to see San Francisco and now it looked as though she would have an opportunity.

Out here I am more or less my own boss reporting direct to the same office I was in in Chicago. I am still in the commercial end and it is my job to secure a haul for the New York Central on as much business or from my territory as possible. Under competitive conditions all the railroads maintain "off-line" offices at various points. The territory under my jurisdiction consists of the northern two thirds of California and the entire state of Nevada. In area it is about seven hundred miles north and south and an equal distance east and west. Needless to say, it will entail quite a bit of travelling. To help me cover this area I have two canvassers whose names appear on the letterhead and for whom I am responsible. In the office are two clerks whom I share with the passenger department.

I feel quite happy about the position because this gives me an official capacity and also more direct responsibility than I have had before. Prior to this I was always under some one else to whom I could go for advice and who was responsible for me. Now I am the head man in my little bailiwick with my nearest superior two thousand miles away. Moreover this is one of the most important "off-line" posts as the territory includes the principal lettuce and grape producing areas in the country. Last year fifty per cent of the entire lettuce shipped in the entire country came from the Salinas district which is under this territory. To date this year there have been 19337 cars of lettuce shipped from that one district going all over the entire country, New York, of course being the principal market. As an indication of what I have to aim at last year our company secured a haul on 15,283 cars of freight originating under the jurisdiction of the San Francisco office of which the principal commodities were:

Fresh Vegetables	5619 cars
Grapes	3172 "
Other Fruit	1720 "
Lumber	1222 "
Canned Goods	1048 "
Wine	883 "
Dried Fruit	563 "

So if the political and international situation will only quiet down I can be very happy.

Please convey my sincerest good wishes to Marjory and I know that if Virginia were here she would join me in wishing you both the best of luck.

Very sincerely yours,

Wally

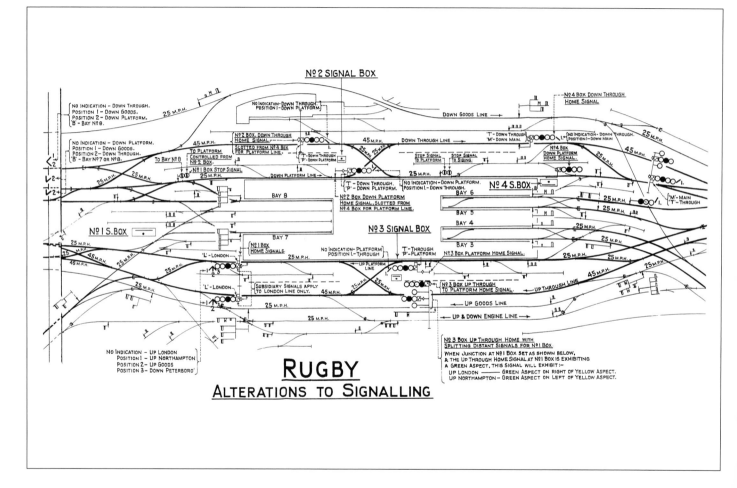

RUGBY
ALTERATIONS TO SIGNALLING

Rugby, Royalty and Tragedy

LONDON MIDLAND AND SCOTTISH RAILWAY COMPANY.
(WESTERN DIVISION.)

SPECIAL NOTICE

THIS NOTICE MUST BE KEPT STRICTLY PRIVATE, AND MUST NOT BE GIVEN TO THE PUBLIC.

NOTICE TO DRIVERS, GUARDS, SIGNALMEN AND OTHERS RESPECTING THE INTRODUCTION OF COLOUR LIGHT SIGNALS (IN PLACE OF EXISTING SEMAPHORE SIGNALS) ON THE UP AND DOWN MAIN LINES THROUGH RUGBY STATION.

Commencing at 2.30 a.m. on Sunday, June 25, the existing mechanical semaphore signalling on the up and down passenger lines at Rugby will be dispensed with and multiple aspect colour light signalling introduced as shown on the attached diagram. Until completion of work flagmen will be provided and trains handsignalled as required. Block Telegraph Signalling will be suspended as necessary.

New trap points, worked from No. 5 signal box, will be brought into use situated in the up line to Nos. 5 and 6 bays about 140 yards from No. 5 signal box.

A new two-armed dwarf shunting signal worked from No. 5 signal box will be provided at the trap points, the top arm reading to down main, down through or down goods loop No. 2, the bottom arm reading to up main or up through (Limit of shunt).

Certain of the running lines will be renamed. The new names are shown on the diagram.

Clifton Road Junction signal box will cease to signal the up Northampton, up and down London and up London goods line.

Except as shown in the following list of signal alterations, new colour light signals superseding the existing semaphore signals will be provided in approximately the same position as the semaphore signals :—

Existing Signal.	Altered or New Signal.
Clifton Road Junction signal box down London line distant.	Superseded by a colour light signal fixed 300 yards nearer Hillmorton Sidings signal box and will become the down distant signal for Clifton Road (down London line) intermediate block home signal and outer distant signal for No. 1 signal box.
Clifton Road Junction signal box down London line home.	Superseded by a colour light signal fixed 290 yards nearer Hillmorton Sidings signal box and will become Clifton Road (down London line) intermediate block home signal controlled from No. 1 signal box.

The demands of war switched Nash back from crystal gazing the future for the LMS to day to day operations at a pivotal location: Rugby. This took place in early 1940, which is indicated on three fronts. The LMS February 1940 report shown two chapters previously is marked for his new post and a letter from Wally Snow at the end of January 1940 congratulates William on becoming the assistant district controller (Rugby). A key letter written to a Swansea friend in July 1940 confirms the date. Technically he was unfit owing to an eyesight condition which had been found in a health check but the war overruled that.

Investment in new signalling was not generally on the wartime agenda but a scheme at Rugby had only been completed in the summer of 1939. Nash was bound to be interested in signalling and a small pile of LMS Special Notices about Signalling schemes has survived. That for Rugby (*an extract of which appears opposite*) is one such and having seen modern equivalents one is struck by the sheer quality of the print for such a notice. The innovation of this scheme was the replacement of mechanical semaphores with four aspect colour lights. Mechanical signalling was retained away from the up and down passenger lines and the co-existence of the two types of signal can be seen in the diagram.

Later in the war, Nash would write memoranda about the Rugby signalling.

Notwithstanding the war some new colour lights were installed and another one of these documents covers the main line between Willesden No. 7 and North Wembley for February 1942 (*overleaf*). Similar wartime notices cover Camden No. 2 to Euston No. 4 and Wigan (NW) and Wigan (Wallgate). All the printing is to the quality of the pre-war item.

North Wembley to Willesden.

Introduction of Colour Light Signalling on Fast & Slow Lines.

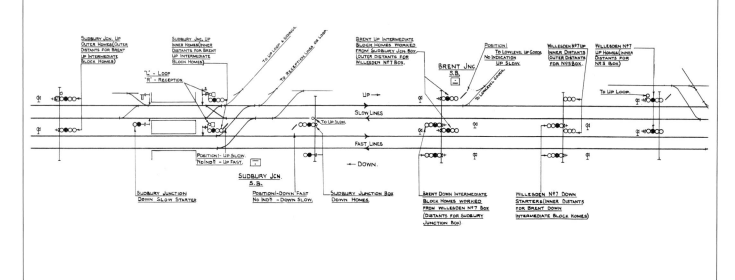

SUDBURY JCN. UP OUTER HOMES (OUTER DISTANTS FOR BRENT UP INTERMEDIATE BLOCK HOMES)

SUDBURY JNC. UP INNER HOMES (INNER DISTANTS FOR BRENT UP INTERMEDIATE BLOCK HOMES)

"L" - LOOP
"R" - RECEPTION

TO UP LOOP & SIDINGS.

TO RECEPTION LINES OR LOOP.

BRENT UP INTERMEDIATE BLOCK HOMES WORKED FROM SUDBURY JCN. BOX. (OUTER DISTANTS FOR WILLESDEN No.7 BOX.)

POSITION I
TO LOWLEVEL UP GOODS
NO INDICATION
UP SLOW.

BRENT JNC S.B.

TO LOWLEVEL GOODS.

WILLESDEN No.7 UP INNER DISTANTS (OUTER DISTANTS FOR No.5 BOX)

WILLESDEN No.7 UP HOMES (INNER DISTANTS FOR No.5 BOX)

TO UP LOOP.

UP →

SLOW LINES

TO UP SLOW.

FAST LINES

POSITION I - UP SLOW.
NO IND.S - UP FAST.

SUDBURY JCN. S.B.

POSITION I - DOWN FAST
NO IND.S - DOWN SLOW.

← DOWN.

SUDBURY JUNCTION DOWN SLOW STARTER

SUDBURY JUNCTION BOX DOWN HOMES.

BRENT DOWN INTERMEDIATE BLOCK HOMES WORKED FROM WILLESDEN No.7 BOX (DISTANTS FOR SUDBURY JUNCTION BOX).

WILLESDEN No.7 DOWN STARTERS (INNER DISTANTS FOR BRENT DOWN INTERMEDIATE BLOCK HOMES)

After the war Nash returned to the Chief Commercial Manager's Office at Euston. In November 1946 he completed another report for the Commercial Office. His brief was to come up with suggestions for dealing with the chronic overloading on the London, Tilbury and Southend section. One of its features was an examination of a proposed 12 mile loop line from Pitsea to Southend East. He was working in the context where it was felt that the wartime exodus of worker residences out of London would become permanent and that a growth of satellite towns was likely. Whether it was the effect of war, but Nash is uncharacteristically reticent about electrification for this route although it was the solution adopted in 1961.

The issue of overcrowding and lack of post-war housing affected the Nashes personally for on returning to the temporary LMS headquarters at The Grove, Watford in late 1945, they had to share their own house in Watford with a family who had rented it during the war. This situation lasted, unpleasantly, for over a year. Four adults and three children were sharing an ordinary three bedroom semi-detached house.

His interest in Esperanto continued; New Year's Greetings for 1950 included a card from Buenos Aires.

By 1950 Nash was once again back in the Euston Square headquarters. He was working in the office of the District Operating Superintendent, Mr L.W. Cox. Apparently his work included the organisation of special events. One memento of this period survives. It is the detailed 24 pages of printed arrangements explaining how the railway would deal with the 1950 Royal Agricultural Society's Show at Oxford (*see overleaf*). Although some way from home, Nash was back on familiar territory near Radley College and the line on which he had considered the potential for the pre-war LMS express diesel railcar. A document like this is a window on a past age when plans were committed to print: a list of cranes to be provided was included along with the details of six special offices to be opened in the period before and during the show.

His final move took place about a year before the Harrow tragedy into Mr Sydney H. Gould's office. Gould answered to Mr S.G. Hearn the Operating Superintendent of the London Midland Region. In this context Nash became responsible for organising Royal Trains and other prestigious movements. One of Nash's colleagues then was Alan Sutcliffe and he writes 'at the time of his death, it was said that Bill would no doubt have moved on to become Chief of one of the Train Planning Offices at Crewe, Derby or Manchester'. It is Alan who has identified William Nash's final position as Senior Clerk Passenger Services in the Chief Operating Superintendent's Office.

5. EVENTS WITHIN THE SHOW GROUND.

Description.	Date/Dates held.
Parade of Heavy Horses	July 5th Morning
Parade of Light Horses	,, ,, ,,
Cattle Parade	,, ,, Afternoon
Tractor Parade	,, ,, ,,
Heythrop Foxhounds Parade	,, ,, ,,
Musical Rides and Activity—Metropolitan Police	,, ,, ,,
Jumping Competitions Nos. 1 and 2	,, ,, ,,
Parade of Heavy Horses	July 6th Morning
Cattle Parade	,, ,, Afternoon
Tractor Parade	,, ,, ,,
Bicester Foxhounds Parade	,, ,, ,,
Musical Rides and Activity—Metropolitan Police	,, ,, ,,
Jumping Competition No. 3	,, ,, ,,
Parade of Heavy Horses	July 7th Morning
Parade of Heavy Draught Teams..	,, ,, ,,
Tractor Parade	,, ,, ,,
Cattle Parade	,, ,, Afternoon
Musical Ride, Metropolitan Police	,, ,, ,,
South Oxfordshire Hounds Parade	,, ,, ,,
Jumping Competitions Nos. 4 and 5	,, ,, ,,

6. DATES OF PRINCIPAL SHOWS BEFORE AND AFTER THE ROYAL SHOW.

Three Counties	Leominster.	June 13th/14th/15th.
Royal Highland	Paisley.	June 20th/21st/22nd/23rd.
Lincolnshire Agricultural	Stamford.	June 21st/22nd.
Royal Counties	Bognor Regis.	June 21st/22nd/23rd/24th.
Royal Norfolk	Wolferton.	June 28th/29th.
Great Yorkshire..	Malton.	July 11th/12th/13th.
Kent County	Maidstone.	July 12th/13th.
Royal Cornwall	Callington.	July 12th/13th.
Bedfordshire	Bedford.	July 14th/15th.
Peterborough Agricultural	Peterborough.	July 18th/19th/20th.
Tunbridge Wells and S.E. Counties ..	Tunbridge Wells.	July 18th/19th.

7. RAIL FACILITIES.

Class of Traffic.	Where Dealt with.
(a) Passengers	Oxford W.R. and Oxford L.M.R. Passenger Stations. Kidlington, Blenheim & Woodstock and Handborough Stations.
(b) Livestock and other Exhibits at Coaching rates requiring floatage. By ordinary train :—	
Horses, Sheep, Cattle, etc., in vehicle loads	Oxford W.R. and Oxford L.M.R. Stations.
Other Exhibits in vehicle loads	ditto
Exhibits in less than vehicle loads	ditto
By Special Train	ditto
(c) Livestock and other Exhibits at Coaching rates not requiring floatage	Kidlington or Handborough as consigned.
(d) Articles exceeding 6 tons in weight requiring cranage	Oxford L.M.R. Goods Yard.
(e) Traffic requiring end-on dock facilities for unloading and loading ..	
By Passenger Train	Oxford W.R. and L.M.R. Stations
By Goods Train	Oxford L.M.R.
(f) Show Goods traffic loaded along with ordinary traffic	Oxford W.R. Goods Station.
(g) Full Wagon loads of Goods traffic	Oxford L.M.R. Goods Yard.

8. OXFORD W.R. PASSENGER STATION ENQUIRY OFFICE AND L.M.R. STATION BOOKING OFFICE.

Enquiry Offices at each Station will be open until 10.30 p.m. from 4th July to 7th, inclusive.

9. RESTRICTIONS ON CATTLE WAGON CLEANING, OXFORD W.R.

Dirty cattle wagons must not be sent to Oxford W.R. for cleaning from 19th June to the 29th July.

10. WEIGHING.

A Cart weighbridge is available as follows :—

    W.R. Top Yard .. ..   Capacity 20-tons.   18 ft. Plate.

11. CRANE POWER.

Where provided.	Crane.
Oxford L.M.R. Yard	6-ton Mobile.
	6-ton Mobile.
Showground	3 X 6-ton Coles Mobile.
	6-ton Thorneycroft Mobile.
	3-ton " Jumbo " Mobile.

12. CRANAGE CHARGES—SHOWGROUND.

Cranage required for the delivery or collection of rail-borne traffic by railway teams will be performed without charge.

For any additional cranage service, at the request of the Trader, the following charges will be levied :—

Rail-borne Traffic.

    6-ton crane — 25/- per hour.   Minimum charge 12/6d.
    3-ton crane — 12/6 ,, ,,   ,, ,, 6/6d.
    (These charges will also apply to rail-borne traffic carted by consignees.)

Non-Rail-borne Traffic.

    6-ton crane — 50/- per hour.   Minimum charge 25/-.
    3-ton crane — 25/- ,, ,,   ,, ,, 13/-.

Application by Traders for the use of the cranes must be referred to the Clerk-in-Charge on the Showground.

Details of all work done must be carefully recorded and the Clerk-in-Charge will arrange for raising of all charges.

13. SPECIAL OFFICE ACCOMMODATION.

Name and Location of Office.	By whom used.	When opened.
Show Goods Office, Oxford L.M.R. Yard ..	Commercial (Goods and Cartage).	Monday, June 12th
Livestock Office, Oxford L.M.R. Yard ..	Commercial and Operating (Livestock and Parcels).	Monday, June 26th
District Officers' Local Liaison Office, Station Master's Office, Oxford W.R.	Joint Commercial and Operating.	Monday, June 19th
Livestock Booking and Parcels Office, Showground ..	Commercial and Operating.	Monday, June 26th
Showground Main Office	Commercial.	Monday, June 12th
Showground Kiosks	Commercial.	Monday, July 3rd.

West Herts Post
and Watford Newsletter

No. 3388 THURSDAY, OCTOBER 16, 1952 Registered as a Newspaper for transmission in the United Kingdom and Abroad. 3d.

The Town Of Mourning

DEATH ROLL–30 : INJURED–52

"Money For Aid Was Placed At Once At The Mayor's Disposal"

FROM all over the world messages have come to Watford conveying the sincere sympathy of good friends.

The town's death roll in the Harrow train smash rose to 30 with Monday's news that two more of the injured had failed to survive. That is 30 of a total of 111 dead, and with 52 injured as well Watford has taken the full impact of tragedy.

But has taken it on the chin; and nobody could better state the stoicism of bereaved families than our Mayor, Ald. L. C. Johnson, when he told a hushed Council on Monday:

" A very tragic Watford, but a very courageous and a very heroic Watford."

This special meeting of the Borough Council was short, dignified and moving. Members spoke simply, obviously greatly affected by the town's tragedy.

The Mayor, Ald. L. C. Johnson, reported that he had visited the bereaved and written to the injured. He had been to the Peace Memorial Hospital to visit an American lady injured in the crash. She had been on her way back to America and a near relative, probably her husband, was in Edgware Hospital. The Mayor said he had written to the lady's relatives in Wigan so they could communicate with her family in Michigan.

COURAGE

The facilities of the Town Hall had been placed at the disposal of the bereaved and injured.

Referring to his visits to the bereaved, the Mayor said, "For courage and fortitude I have never seen the like. One went there to minister to them. One felt when one came away one had been ministered to."

He paid tribute to the work of local clergymen particularly the Rev. E. D. P. Kelsey, Vicar of the badly-hit Christ Church.

" A very tragic Watford but a very courageous and a very heroic Watford," commented the Mayor.

The facilities of the Town Hall had been placed at the disposal of the bereaved and injured.

Referring to his visits to the bereaved, the Mayor said, "For courage and fortitude I have never seen the like. One went there to minister to them. One felt when one came away one had been ministered to."

He paid tribute to the work of local clergymen—particularly the Rev. E. D. P. Kelsey, Vicar of the badly-hit Christ Church.

" A very tragic Watford but a very courageous and a very heroic Watford," commented the Mayor.

Letters had been received, reported the Mayor, from the Railway Executive—accepting full legal liability for the accident—the chairman of Harrow U.D.C., the Mayor of St. Albans, Reeve Roy Cook, of Watford, Ontario, Mr. John Freeman, Watford's M.P. Mr. Sydney Ripley prospective Conservative Parliamentary candidate for Watford, overseas students who recently visited Watford and from many towns —including Portsmouth, Rochdale, Huddersfield, St. Leonards-on-Sea, Gloucester, Thorpe-le-Soken, Southborough, Glasgow and London.

Cllr. E. J. Baxter said money had been put immediately at the Mayor's disposal for the needs of any of the families affected.

He expressed " the deepest possible sympathy for all those people who are bereaved."

THE LESSON

Cllr. L. D. White wondered if the Council could not learn something from their feelings about the tragedy. " It does seem to me to take something of this nature to really unite us. In our forms of government we are bound to have differences of opinion, but can't we take a lesson from this. Can't we keep out some of this bitterness which does creep in ? "

Cllr. T. F. Harris said he had known many of the victims personally. " The tragedy is these young people should be cut off in the very flower of their lives."

Like the Mayor, he referred specially to the work of the Rev. Kelsey.

Deputy Mayor Ald. L. E. Haines recalled that in 1912 there had been a somewhat similar accident—a train from Watford had been run into from the rear.

" Everyone of us would wish to give every assistance we can," he added.

Ald. H. Horwood praised the fortitude of the bereaved and the number of people who had come forward volunteering assistance.

That was really all there was to say. All week the town has demonstrated its real sympathy and desire to help the bereaved families. The grieved friends who have attended the funerals have been condolence for the relatives.

There Were 800 On That Local Train, Inquiry Told

WHEN the public inquiry into the triple train crash opened at Euston yesterday, the Inspector was told that there were 800 people on the local Tring-Euston train.

Train adjustments caused the rush for it, and that is why there were more Watford people aboard than usual.

Lieut.-Col. G. R. S. Wilson, Chief Inspecting Officer of Railways, opened the inquiry. After an omnibus vote of thanks to all the rescue workers of voluntary organisations, and especially the American unit, he went on to say that the inquiry was held primarily from the technical aspects of the case so the Minister could be advised of the cause of the accident and know any steps which should be taken to prevent other accidents.

It was by no means a court of inquiry into the legal responsibility of the railways or any of their employees.

WORLD SYMPATHY

Messages of sympathy had been received from all over the world, said Mr. J. W. Watkins, Chief Regional Officer. There was one from the Government of Yugoslavia.

A railway official gave a summary of the accident. The total of killed was 111. Of these, 108 were passengers and three were members of engine crews. 167 people were taken to hospital; eight of them had since died. 69 had been discharged after treatment. 37 of the killed and 98 of the injured were railway employees. 74 people were still in hospital, six of them seriously ill.

There were 800 passengers on the local train, 90 in the Perth express, and 186 on the Liverpool express. The local trains were more heavily loaded than normal because of train adjustments.

MISTY MORNING

After the technical preamble with which the inquiry opened, first witness was Charles Sidney Romminson, the Harrow stationmaster, who said that he had been at Harrow for about two years.

Asked about weather conditions on the morning of the crash, he said it was not foggy when he came on duty at 8 o'clock but misty and patchy in places.

At 8.10 he came out of the booking office in order to go to his own office. He did not look towards the signal box. He was concerned about visibility on his way in from his home to the station but when he reached the station he thought it was not going to be such a bad morning after all.

He could see for a couple of hundred yards.

He was on No. 4 platform when the local train from Tring

ITS SCOPE

MINISTER of Transport Mr. Lennox-Boyd was asked in the House of Commons on Tuesday whether yesterday's inquiry would be wide enough in its scope to cover the general questions of safety devices used by the railways, or which could be used in the case of human or mechanical failure in operation.

He replied: " I feel sure that the scope of the inquiry can be safely left in the competent hands of my Chief Inspector of Accidents."

came in six or seven minutes late, arriving at 8.17. He believed the train had got away in two minutes. When the first collision took place he was near the first coach.

To him it did not seem a serious accident at first. A matter of seconds—not more than twenty or so—and the Manchester train came into the station.

He did not think the driver could see anything at the time. He did not hear the brakes go on. When the Tring train had been folled he realised something serious had happened and he ran.

TEARING NOISE

" It sounded to me like a tearing noise, as though someone had left a compartment door open and it had been caught by the engine," he said.

He ran for a telephone, and as he ran he saw the bridge go, cutting him off from his office.

The collision was at 8.18, and ten minutes later he was in the signal box.

He did not take particular notice of the signal north, but he could see the one to the south, which was 200 yards away. The signalman was deathly white, and he took him out on to the steps for air.

Witness said he did not know the signalman very well. He was a relief signalman who had only been there a few days previously. During this time he had been perfectly satisfied with his work.

Witness said he knew that the signalman was allowed to work with a visibility of 200 yards.

When witness came on duty he was satisfied that conditions were workable, as it was only patchy fog.

BUSHEY WITNESS

Mr. H. E. Foskett, of Bushey, station foreman at Harrow and Wealdstone station, said he came on duty at 6 a.m.

The earlier trains were running " reasonably to time."

He was on the platform at the bottom of the footbridge when the Tring train was in the station.

Normally about 20 to 30 people get off the train at Harrow and about 300 get on. They had not all got on at the time of the accident.

About the collision between the Perth express and the Tring train, he said: " I did not even know an accident had happened. I never got the noise. As far as I was concerned the truck has tilted forward, there was an escape of steam and then the coach came up at me."

He went to a public phone box and dialled 999. He told the operator " Get as many ambulances, police and doctors as quickly as you can." He said there was a "machine-gun effect " as the Manchester express rattled along the coaches of the Tring train.

THE SIGNALMAN

Signalman H. E. Horsfall, of 26, Milton-street, Watford, said that he booked on duty at six o'clock on the morning. It was foggy, but visibility was 300 yards. When he went on duty he did

(Continued on Back Page)

MR. A. HINE

of 36, Thorpe-crescent, Watford, 20 years old, was fireman on the 8.01 Tring-Euston train. He is pictured with his mother, Mrs. Audrey Hine, and their dog Skipper. Mr. Hine escaped unhurt from the crash, but suffered from delayed shock. Next day he was at work as usual with a new driver.

Council Offer Of Help

WATFORD BOROUGH COUNCIL at a special meeting on Monday evening, passed this resolution:

" The Council places on record its most sincere regret at the triple rail disaster which occurred on the morning of October 8 at Harrow and Wealdstone station, resulting as it did in a serious loss of life and injury to a large number of the passengers, including many of the townspeople of Watford. The Council records its expression of profound condolence with the bereaved relatives.

" The Council associates itself with the action taken by the Mayor in visiting the relatives of those who were killed . . . and in writing to those who were injured, expressing hope for a speedy recovery.

" The Council expresses its desire to help in any practical way the relatives of deceased and seriously injured persons and to give advice where this is sought."

THE TOWN'S TRIBUTE

Watford's memorial service for those killed in the rail disaster will be at St Mary's Parish Church at 3 p.m. on Sunday, October 26. The Lord Bishop of St. Albans has promised to preach, reported the Mayor, Ald. L. C. Johnson, at Monday's special council meeting.

Members of the various services who assisted at the crash will attend.

Junction A Terminus

FOR a time, Watford Junction became a railway terminus last week-end.

When the line was blocked at Harrow, some trains were stopped at the Junction and their passengers re-directed into London by other routes. A fleet of buses ran a regular service from the Junction to the Met. station.

But after the first few hours most of the trains were diverted further up the line to St. Pancras and Paddington.

"We resumed normal working on Saturday," said a spokesman at the Junction. "The schedule was thrown out of gear, and naturally it meant a certain amount

The dreadful manner whereby Nash lost his life while commuting to the LMR Euston Head Office was explored in some detail in *Cumbrian Railway Photographer* (and also in another Oakwood title published at the same time in 2002, *Harrow & Wealdstone 50 Years On*). What can be added is a glance at two items still with the family. The first are extracts from the front page of the *West Herts Post and Watford Newsletter* for Thursday 16th October, 1952. The 30 figure refers to the town of Watford's own loss which was where William Nash then lived.

The second is an item of very restricted circulation and will have been seen but rarely. Accordingly our volume closes by reproducing whole the printed text of the address given at the Harrow Disaster memorial service. This took place at St Marylebone Parish Church and was by the Lord Bishop of Stepney, the Rt Revd Joost de Blank. It can stand as a memorial along with his photos to William Nash and everyone else who lost their lives on that foggy October morning.

Text of the Address by the LORD BISHOP of Stepney,
The Rt. Rev. Joost de Blank at the

MEMORIAL SERVICE

for those Railway Employees whose lives were lost in the railway accident at Harrow & Wealdstone Station on 8th October, 1952

and

SERVICE OF THANKSGIVING

for those whose lives were spared.

THURSDAY, 23rd OCTOBER, 1952

at 11.30 a.m.

—

ST. MARYLEBONE PARISH CHURCH
LONDON, W.1

Whether we live or die we are the Lord's—Romans 14-8

The railway accident at Harrow and Wealdstone station occurred on the morning of October 8th, now over a fortnight ago. The numbing effect of the first dreadful shock is just beginning to disperse ; perhaps because of that we are more conscious of our grief today, its pain more bitter, but also we can think about the disaster a little more completely, a little more objectively. That, I am sure, is the reason why those who planned this service have, as you see on the cover page of the papers you have in your hand, coupled with this Memorial Service, a Service of Thanksgiving. " Thanksgiving "—the word does not come easily to our lips at such a time, and yet it is on the note of thanksgiving that I wish to dwell this morning, and that in no way to minimise the enduring grief and prayerful sympathy we all feel for those many, many people who have been so suddenly bereaved.

First then this is a Service of Thanksgiving for the faithful work rendered by those who work on our railways. Day in, day out, night after night, month after month, year after year many thousands of men combine to criss-cross our country with efficient passenger and freight transport services. We tend to take it all so much for granted. We grumble if our train is a little late, if our compartment is a bit dusty, if we miss a promised connection ; we all do because we all want perfection, and it is a tribute to our railways and their staff that we expect perfection. We would not bother to grumble were it not for the fact that the great tradition of our railways leads us to be satisfied with nothing less than punctuality, cleanliness, speedy communication and the like. It is a sad commentary on our human insensitiveness that we can settle down into our seat in the train and take all this for granted, with never a thought for all the painstaking work on the part of so many people to make our journey possible, and equally to plan our programme in the expectation that our train will carry us to our destination safely and promptly. Not till we are shaken out of our apathetic acceptance of this faithful untiring service do we remember with gratitude those who day after day bring us smoothly to our journey's end. So now we want to thank them all, now we want to thank God for their ceaseless devotion to duty, now we are shamed —all of us—that we remember them so seldom in our prayers.

But on this occasion we would specially give thanks for the heroic courage and endurance and self-forgetfulness of all railway folk who in any sense shared in the rescue work at Wealdstone. We render our homage to all the citizens who did what they could, to the clergy and ministers, the police, hospital and ambulance services, to the men and women working with the United States Forces, to all the local agencies—our praise and gratitude can never fully be expressed—but here I would dwell on the men of the railways themselves. It so happens that the 7.31 Tring to Euston train always carries many railwaymen on their way to work, and it is not generally known that more than a third of those who died as a result of the accident were railway employees—43 out of 112—while nearly two-thirds of those in hospital, 114 out of 181 are railwaymen or railwaywomen. Yet in spite of the terrific shock, those railwaymen and railwaywomen who were travelling in the train and were fortunate enough to be uninjured, at once, without a moment's hesitation, set about relief work and by the time the first ambulance arrived, only four minutes after the crash, they had already organised themselves on the lines of an A.R.P. Post and there is no doubt that this prompt action saved many lives.

Perhaps now we begin to understand better why this dares to be called a Service of Thanksgiving. We proved the dauntless heroism of our railways during the war ; for you might say we were all keyed up together then. But at Wealdstone when disaster came so tragically and unexpectedly immediately the same heroism, the same selfless concern for others, the same loyalty and duty were shown and we give our thanks to all concerned and we give our thanks to Almighty God for making such men as match the hour of our distress.

There are other reasons why the word Thanksgiving does not come amiss this morning. This is a Service of Thanksgiving for our Christian hope. How sadly we enumerate the number that have been killed, how we feel for all those who are passing through the agony of sorrow and of loneliness. We do not ask them to suppress their grief, to restrain their tears—for as human beings we have been given the capacity for love and though love is not finally dependent on it, yet how much it values the touch of the hand, the sound of the voice which now have been tragically snatched from us. For the Christian hope does not deny the anguish of separation, it accepts the Cross with all its pain—but it asserts that the separation is not final, that the Cross can lead on to Resurrection. We sometimes sing, " O Joy that seekest me through pain, I cannot close my heart to thee, I trace the rainbow through the rain, and feel the promise is not vain, that morn shall tearless be." We trace the rainbow through the rain—and we look beyond our present distress to that joyful Resurrection and Reunion.

I remember once seeing a signpost pointing up a village lane which said " No road past the cemetery." It came as a shock to see those words, and though true of the geography of that village wholly untrue in terms of life and death. " No road past the cemetery" indeed! Of course there is—a high road driven through the line of graves and at its entrance this banner in gold letters, " I am the Resurrection and the Life, saith the Lord." When we suddenly are thrust away from someone very dear to us, is that the end when you and he had promised that your love would never die? And your love for Christ is that to end with death ? No. He has promised, " I go to prepare a place for you and if I go I will come again and receive you unto myself that where I am there ye may be also."

In this faith countless men and women have lived and died. Let me give you just one example of a man who died in the cause of duty as so many whom we mourn today. I refer to Dr. Edward Wilson who died with Captain Scott in the Antarctic 40 years ago. In his last letter to his wife he wrote " We are playing a good part in a great scheme arranged by God Himself and all is well. We have struggled to the end but the Great Ice Barrier has beaten us. My beloved wife, these are small things and life itself is a small thing to me now, but my love for you is for ever, and a part of our love for God. All the things I had hoped to do with you after this expedition are as nothing now, but we will meet after death, and there are greater things for us to do in the world to come. All is well." In our own circumstances we echo those words—and so this is a Service of Thanksgiving for we do not sorrow as men without hope for them that sleep in Jesus. For the moment the curtain has fallen between us, but one day it will be raised and we shall be more together than ever before. Such men and women who have been snatched from us, faithful in their duty and their love, such people do not die, they only change their address.

There is still one more reason why this is a Service of Thanksgiving. We give our grateful thanks for those whose lives were spared. Story upon story has come to us of people who intended to travel by one or other of those three trains but did not or were prevented by one reason or another. A young railwayman in my own old parish travelled up regularly with that train on every day except Wednesday — and many report similar providences. In this church this morning there must be those who are giving thanks that their loved ones were not in the trains, or that they escaped death or serious injury, or thank God that at least they are alive. And there must be those who are grateful that though involved in the accident, while others suffered they are here. There were many employees on the train who are not among the 43 that were killed. And though for Christians death has not the horror and finality that it has for those who have no faith—yet we give God thanks that our family circle is unbroken, that we have been spared to continue our lives here below a little longer.

Let us at all events be quite clear of this that we are not spared because of any special virtue in us. There is nothing in religion that can shield us from what the world calls trouble, there is no Christian promise that we shall not suffer accident or disaster. But when tragedy overtakes our friends and we are left unwounded —" it is then that the presence cf the Son of Man is felt : then is the day of our merciful and mysterious deliverance." How easy it is for us normally to take life and all that it gives us for granted, and we grow self-sufficient and arrogant—but on a day like this we make our thanksgiving because we have been shaken into an awareness of the eternal realities. There is among us " a strength not our own, beyond anything that we possess of our own " and " I am immortal till my work is done." Our thanksgiving for the fact that our lives are spared is just a matter of words and no more if it does not recall us to the real meaning of life, if it does not teach us that man is made for God and finds fulfilment only in God. Our thanksgiving is real just insofar as it leads us to a desire to do God's will and walk in His way. If a man lives a holy and humble Christian life there is no pledge that he will not suffer accident, but if he lives in purity and unselfishness death has no more terrors for him for whether he lives or dies he has placed himself trustingly in God's hands.

It is, I know, hard to give thanks in the midst of sorrow, but I most firmly believe that our sorrow will be lessened as we try to be thankful—thankful for the faithful service of the men who man our railways and, in particular, those who worked so valiantly at the time of the accident ; thankful too for our Christian hope, which assures us through the Resurrection of our Lord Jesus Christ from the dead, that death is not the end but that in Christ there is reunion and fulness of life beyond the grave ; thankful too that we have been spared with many known to us and that in our deliverance life's true significance has come home to us and in this most serious moment of our lives we would be what God would have us be.

And so with our thanksgiving we would show further our praise not only with our lips but in our lives. In this catastrophe we recognise that in the midst of life we are in death, and that the one unchanging anchorage in this world and the next is our God Whose Name is Love and who gives Himself to us in His Son Jesus. In fellowship with Him death loses its fears for our fellowship is unbroken with our loved ones and then " whether we live we are the Lord's or whether we die we are the Lord's—whether we live or die therefore we are the Lord's."

Bibliography

Many, many books and magazine articles have been consulted. What might be termed standard works of reference like H.C. Casserley's and S.W. Johnston's *Locomotives at the Grouping* and the David & Charles *Forgotten Railways* series are not individually cited. Publications and features which have been of especial value and/or which may not be widely known will be.

Barnfield, Peter: 'Across Central Wales' in *Railway Bylines*, May 2003.

Brown, G.A., Prideaux, J.D.C., Radcliffe, H.G.: *The Lynton and Barnstaple Railway*, David & Charles, 1971.

Burt, Ronald G.: 'Old Jersey Railways' in *ann.Bull.Soc.jersaise*, 18,1, 1961.

Coster, Peter J.: *The Book of the A3 Pacifics*, Irwell Press, 2003.

Davies, W.J.K.: *The Ravenglass and Eskdale Railway*, David & Charles, 1981.

Essery, R.J., Jenkinson, D.: *An Illustrated Review of Midland Locomotives Volumes 1-4*, Wild Swan, 1984ff.

Ferreira, Douglas: *Ratty's 100, Ravenglass and Eskdale Railway*, 1976.

Hartley, Norman: 'Basingstoke Shed' in *British Railways Illustrated*, October 1993.

Haut, F.J.G.: *The History of the Electric Locomotive*, George Allen & Unwin, 1969.

Hoole, Ken: *North Eastern Locomotive Sheds*, David & Charles, 1972.

Jenner, David; Smith, Adrian; Van Zeller, Peter: *The Ravenglass & Eskdale Railway A Journey Through Historic Postcards*, Ravenglass & Eskdale Railway, 1991.

Judge, C.: *Railways of the Channel Islands*, Oakwood Press, 1992.

Milner, W.J.: *Rails Through The Sand*, Rail Romances, 1996.

Pealling, Colin: 'William Nash, Photographer' in *Lynton & Barnstaple Railway Magazine*, Spring 2003.

Plant, Ken: *The Ashover Light Railway*, Oakwood Press, 1987.

Richards, E. V.: *LMS Diesel Locomotives and Railcars*, RCTS, 1996.

Russell, J.H.: *A Pictorial Record of Great Western Engines, Volumes One and Two*, Oxford Publishing Company, 1975.

Smith, Martin: 'Weymouth Quay' in *British Railways Illustrated*, February-March 1993.

Strong, Paul: '100 years of a Cotswold railway line Parts 1 and 2' in *Backtrack*, Nov.-Dec. 1992 and Jan.-Feb. 1993.

Summers, L.A.: 'The Great Western's 'Bonniest' Engines' (M&SWJR 4-4-0s) in *Backtrack*, September 2000.

Tatlow, Peter: *Harrow Railway Disaster - 50 Years On - Clearing up the Aftermath*, Oakwood Press, 2002.

Turner, Keith: *The Leek & Manifold Valley Light Railway*, David & Charles, 1980.

Vaughan, A.: *Great Western Portrait 1913-1921*, Oxford Publishing Company, 1971.

Vaughan, A.: *The Kenning Collection*, Oxford Publishing Company, 1972.

Yeadon, Willie B.: *A Compendium of LNWR Locomotives 1912-1949* Part One Passenger Tender Engines, Challenger Publications, 1995.

Index

The index is principally to the photographs and does not include text references to the individual locations shown. Within each of the four main grouped companies, constituent companies are listed, regardless of whether the image is pre- or post-Grouping. The entries solely listed beside the grouped company refer to an entry whose content is derived only from post-Grouping activity.